IT'S ONLY
THE
BEGINNING

It's Only the Beginning

A journey with Jesus

Kim Kollins
with John Patrick Grace

HIGHLAND BOOKS

ISBN 0 946616 56 6

Cover design: Diane Drummond

Cover photograph: Ed Bergwerff

Scripture quotations marked KJV
are from the *King James Version*
of the Bible. Scripture quotations
marked RSV are from the *Revised
Standard Version* of the Bible.

Printed in Great Britain for
HIGHLAND BOOKS
Broadway House, The Broadway
Crowborough, East Sussex TN6 1BY
by Richard Clay Ltd, Bungay, Suffolk
Typeset by Rowland Phototypesetting Ltd,
Bury St Edmunds, Suffolk

To Robert and Darin, my sons
with love, and thanks for living it all with me

Acknowledgments

I would like to thank Frère Ephraim of the Lion of Juda community for his support in the publishing of this book and in my ministry to so many of the community's houses. Also for personal and helpful suggestions, comfort and, in some instances, hospitality as a 'writer in residence', I am indebted to: Philippe and Jill Maucorps and their son, Martin; Fr Doctor Nobert Baumert, SJ; Fr Michael Marsch, OP; Fr Ken Metz; my first pastor, the Rev Marvin Crow; Anita Schulz; Jennifer Grace and Claude and Cathy Brenti.

Contents

Foreword

It is only comparatively recently that Kim Kollins has become well-known, particularly in Europe, where she is a talented ambassador for Christ. Having myself been involved in a leadership role in the European charismatic scene for many years, I can vouch for the integrity that Kim brings to all she says and does.

Kim has been through many troubled waters. She was born into a Lutheran family but as a child also attended a Baptist church. She fell away from the faith for nearly twenty years and has now become a Roman Catholic. My experience has been that most people who make this journey find relating back to their past extremely difficult. Not so with Kim. Her vision remains the unity of the whole Body of Christ, and I have always found her to possess a Christ-like empathy with members of all churches. Her vision of the unity of the Body of Christ is not based on mere sentimentality or words, it is part of her; and she lives it day by day.

The story of Kim's life is fascinating, and I was gripped by it when I read it. Her call to Europe, and her ability to become European is perhaps the most important clue to this story. She has learnt to be 'all things to all men' and to respect cultural differences without becoming anti-American.

There is a great need in our times for female leadership. I see some women trying to be leaders and imitating the men in doing so. It does not work. The male characteristics of leadership need to be complemented by something which is distinctly feminine. Kim's leadership is just that, and her contribution in situations which still seem to be male dominated has been important. One is reminded of the saying that when God wants something difficult to be done, he chooses a man; when something impossible, he chooses a woman! Kim is just such a woman, and my prayer is that this book will encourage men and women to honour one another in mutual respect to the glory of God.

Michael Harper

About this book

In September 1977 I started the final phase of my search to rediscover the God of my childhood, a leg of my spiritual journey that would cover nine months and end with my acknowledging Jesus Christ as my Lord and Saviour. I had a sense, even then, that one day I would write a book about my journey and already was keeping notes.

As the Lord launched me into the ministry of an itinerant evangelist, first in Texas and Louisiana, then across wider stretches of the United States and finally into Europe, Africa and Indonesia, I asked myself from time to time, 'Is *now* the moment to write the book?'

Each time I came to see that what I had once conceived as a simple sharing of my personal spiritual journey to God was expanding and becoming more and more complex, in ways I had never contemplated. My journey had taken me from the south-western US to Europe and to two other continents. I had begun as a Christian business executive, then was sent out as an evangelist from the International Christian Centre, an interdenominational church in Garland, Texas. I passed to an association with a contemplative French Catholic monastic community, the Lion of Juda and the Slain Lamb, and to duties as a member of the national service committee of the German Catholic Charismatic Renewal. Finally, I had also been selected to participate in European and international ecumenical charismatic leaders' groups.

My understanding of the Body of Christ deepened as God wove my path in and out of many Christian churches. What also deepened, quite painfully, was my awareness of conflict, prejudice and hatred still present in the Body. I lost my early naïve way of thinking that everyone who believed in Jesus would recognise and love everyone else who believed in him. I had to face the reality that the wounds of centuries of religious strife among Christians were still deep, and a great deal of healing was needed before Jesus' Body on earth could be whole.

No matter where the Lord took me, no matter to what country or into what part of his Body, I always could see Jesus in my brothers and sisters, could feel his love manifested in their midst. I would often ask myself, 'Why is it so difficult for some Christians to see the Lord in other Christians and to receive others *even* in their doctrinal differences?' Perhaps if everybody could have, as I have had, an opportunity to live with brothers and sisters from Christian groups other than their own, *then* they could break through the barriers of their own prejudices.

As I approached the tenth anniversary of my homecoming to the Lord Jesus, I received an intuition that *now* was the time to share my spiritual journey and the story of the ministry to which God had called me. Now was the time for a book.

I knew instinctively, however, that this sharing would be difficult and sometimes even controversial. For some brothers and sisters in the Lord my journey would be very hard to understand. Not wanting to offend any of them, I at first found myself blocked—I could not see how I could tell the story at all. One part of Christ's Body, I could see, might have problems with *this* section of my journey, another part of the Body with *that* section. I almost gave up the project.

However, it was the Holy Spirit, I believe, who urged me to go forward, impressing upon my heart the following scripture: 'For my thoughts are not your thoughts, neither are your ways my ways, saith the Lord' (Isaiah 55.8, KJV). Like Paul I am also aware, that 'we see through a glass darkly' (1 Corinthians 13.12a, KJV), and that our perceptions evolve and deepen as we walk with the Lord. My

present understandings of my walk therefore are not necessarily my final ones, as the Spirit uncovers further layers of
God's revelation.

So in obedience to what I perceive God has been urging
upon me and out of the courage he has instilled in me, I have
risked sharing my personal journey in the Lord the way I
lived it. I am trusting that the Lord our God will bring
understanding to the hearts and minds of all he would draw
to these pages.

Kim Catherine-Marie Kollins

(Different parts of the Body use different terms for doctrine,
practices, rites of worship or ministerial positions. In recounting
my walk I have used the terms used by the various parts of the
Body as I participated in each part. To facilitate understanding I
have put definitions and clarifications of such terms in footnotes.)

I
SEARCH FOR GOD

SEARCH FOR GOD

I was born Phyllis Ann Miller on September 16, 1943, in Mount Clemens, Michigan, USA. My parents were Emily Ann Miller and Philip Joseph Miller. My father was born in 1900 in Pozarevac, Yugoslavia, sixty kilometres south-east of Belgrade, which at that time—before World War I—was part of the Austro-Hungarian empire. My mother was born as Emma Anne Bellmann in 1908 and raised in her birthplace of Buxtehude, Germany, south-west of Hamburg.

Both had immigrated to the United States, my father in the 1920s, my mother in the 1930s. My parents had both had a previous marriage that ended in divorce; I was the only child of their marriage to each other. From my father's first marriage, I have a half-brother and a half-sister, Joseph and Mary.

When he first came to America my father settled in Mansfield, Ohio, and for a time did industrial work; then he began to sell vacuum cleaners door to door, developing this business into a small sales and service company. My mother attended university in Germany and in the United States worked in interior decorating.

My birth came during World War II while my father was working as a civilian in the US military intelligence corp, stationed in Michigan. Several years later my parents moved back to Mansfield, then an industrial town of fifty thousand people. Here I was to live until I was almost twenty-six years old, except for two years in Costa Mesa, California, when I was four and five. My upbringing was simply middle-class American. Our house in Mansfield was undistinguished but adequate. From the time I was seven or eight my parents had a cabin on Lake Erie in which we spent weekends during spring and summer. When I was not sunbathing, swimming or waterskiing, I would often go fishing on the lake with my Dad. In the autumn he would take me rabbit hunting.

I was raised in a very loving atmosphere. A child who was wanted, I was born three years after my parents married. Because of a difficult pregnancy my mother had to stay in bed for the last few months to ensure that I should be born alive. At the time of my birth, during the war, few doctors were readily available. I had started to be born early in the morning and the obstetrics staff gave my mother a shot to try to stop her labour so that her doctor could finish his office hours. My father became very angry, went to the doctor's office, grabbed the doctor by the collar and told him, 'Look, you deliver that baby!' And I was born that afternoon in St Joseph Catholic hospital.

When reflecting on my childhood, I find that I was outgoing, independent, and goal-oriented. I believe I inherited from my parents a natural ability in management and marketing that would later become my profession. This trait soon began to manifest itself. When I was seven my family had a garden with a large strawberry patch behind our house. I would help my father pick strawberries, then take the berries around the neighbourhood and sell them. I also sold Christmas cards and greeting cards in the same way between the ages of eight and ten. As a girl scout I sold cookies door to door and was always one of the girls with the highest sales.

I loved to work just for the challenge of it—not because my family circumstances required it. At fourteen I began my first grown-up job: doing inventory control and payroll for a clothing-store chain, whose home office was in New York. I worked after school and on weekends that spring and then full time in the summer. Continuing in this pattern I spent one year, at age fifteen, as a waitress and the next as a typist in an attorney's office. Despite my working so much in my childhood I also found school an agreeable challenge and got mostly good grades. I also liked sports. In all, I have fond memories of my childhood.

One of the fondest is my recollection of two summers spent in Europe at ages six and twelve, visiting my maternal grandparents in Germany, with a little time in France en route. My grandparents lived in the old section of Buxtehude on Kirchenstrasse, so named because the Lutheran church stood at the end. At the end of my first summer's stay there my mother and I spent ten days in Paris, staying in a hotel on the Champs Elysée, before embarking on a ship for New York. As a souvenir I brought home a miniature glass Eiffel Tower, which I kept in my room for many years. Did I have some childhood intuition that France would play a key role in my future? Perhaps . . .

My parents, it occurs to me as I look back, had a deep and beautiful relationship, which provided a healthy climate for me to blossom into adolescence. Both were Lutheran and I was apparently baptised in a Lutheran church when I was about three months old. I never saw a certificate of baptism, but I remember a picture of my mother holding me in her arms and telling me, 'This is the day you were christened.'

My parents were never active in the Lutheran church. I can recall going to that church several times with my mother, but never with both my parents. In school our class had weekly Bible study, with a woman coming in and telling us Bible stories. During summer various churches around our house held vacation Bible schools,[1] and I went to a number of such sessions. I started confirmation studies in the Lutheran church, but in the second year I stopped going to these classes and never was confirmed Lutheran.

---

[1] Vacation Bible school provides a morning day camp for children for a week or so. It usually includes the telling of Bible stories, production of sketches and biblical arts and crafts projects.

At about this time a new Baptist church started holding services two doors from my home in the basement of the pastor's house while their church building was being erected. I started to go there for youth activities and then encouraged my parents to attend services. They became members by going through a rite of adult baptism.[2] I, however, never did; and so never actually became a member of the Baptist church. (I did not, as a child, have any concept whatsoever about denominations or divisions in the churches.) Nonetheless, I did plunge into many of the church's youth programmes and also sang in the choir.

I can remember sitting in that church listening to the altar call given every Sunday 'for those who want to give their life to Jesus'. I would say under my breath, 'Lord, I want to belong to you. Take my heart.' But the invitation was to come forward and to profess your faith for all to hear, and I never did that. I lived my commitment in my heart but I didn't have the courage to rise and go forward. Still I feel that during that time I *did* enter into a relationship with the Lord; I'm quite sure God responded to that assent in my heart. This went on for two or three years—with an altar call every Sunday.

Between the ages of thirteen and fourteen, however, I slackened off all church activities, including attending Sunday services. Jobs, sports, cheerleading and the cabin on the lake pulled me away from my church life.

---

[2] Baptist churches do not accept infant baptism as valid.

1

1969: On my own

This wandering away from faith had many negative consequences, including, as would soon be evident, devastation of hopes and dreams for a happy married life. So much so that by the year 1969 I found myself divorced and alone with two children, soon to be eight and four, whose financial support was left almost entirely up to me.

At age seventeen, against my parents' wishes, I had married my high-school sweetheart. My first son, Robert Philip, was born into this marriage. After two and a half years the relationship with my husband went awry, and ended in divorce. Shortly afterwards I met a man with whom I firmly hoped I could have a marriage that would last until death. My son, Darin Clinton, was born in the second year of this marriage, and my husband legally adopted my first son, Robert. However, because of a painful series of events that devastated our relationship, I was now, after six years of marriage, once again to find myself having to cope with a divorce.[3]

Shortly before my twenty-sixth birthday I thus entered a time of trying to build a new life for myself and my two sons. Even though I had always worked outside the home during my married life, everything now would be different.

As part of establishing myself in my new role I decided to accept a promotion to the home office of a fast-growing international conglomerate, for whose field operations I had already been working for seven months. The corporation's

---

[3] I had never received any instruction on Christian marriage. Only years afterwards, when I found my way back to the Lord, was I to learn that I had had no concept of what God wanted marriage to be. Both men that I had been married to went on to remarry several years after the divorces. Each has a second family, one with three sons and one with a daughter.

interests spanned everything from cosmetics to real estate. I was named as president of one of the company's national divisions. This meant moving from Ohio, the state of my childhood, to Orlando, Florida.

This new work initially required extensive travel. My parents and I agreed that during this phase it would be good if my children lived with them and stayed in their present schools. This meant seeing my children only four or five days a month, which was very hard for me, but my parents and I believed that this was the most stable solution for them.

Starting a totally new life, beginning with nothing, I left my house and all my furniture back in Ohio for my parents to sell and rented a one-bedroom apartment in Florida. As perhaps another way of adjusting to my situation, I yielded to an inspiration to change my name legally from Phyllis Ann to Kimberly, the name I had chosen for my second baby had it been a girl.

I plunged into my new position with great energy, but soon came to realise that I was trying to lose myself in my work, to numb the pain in my heart from my marital break-up and the separation from my children.

Something else began to happen in that autumn: through business contacts I met many people that had very different spiritual beliefs. Some were Christians, some believers in eastern religions and philosophies and in reincarnation, some followers of astrology, some spiritualists. Some were agnostics, others atheists. This was my first encounter with spiritual beliefs other than Christian ones.

Because I had no knowledge of God's Word, the Bible, I didn't know which areas of spiritual beliefs were of God, which were not. I would listen with interest to them all, but never committed myself to take part in one area or another. Somehow I adopted the understanding that all these approaches to spiritual concepts fitted together; they were, to my mind then, just different avenues of expression of the same reality.

The corporation I worked for had strong ideas in favour of positive thinking. The literature of 'positive thinking' was very popular in America in the 1960s and 1970s. The various books by Napoleon Hill, especially *Think and Grow Rich* and *Principles of Success*, a motivation course, were virtually required reading in this corporation.

Since I had always had a positive attitude to life, I seized upon this material with a will and attempted to develop the positive thinking focus even more. Indeed, I reached a point where I thought that I really did have a great ability to control what was going on in my life—or so I believed.

An employee named Patti Schmidt who worked in our book-keeping department was a 'Spirit-filled' Christian.[4] It was this eighteen-year-old girl, I was to learn much later, whom the Lord was to use to intercede for me. She kept me in her prayers faithfully for years, as my spirit tossed about dangerously in murky seas, desperately looking for its harbour in God's peace and love.

2

Stirrings

In the spring of 1970 I began to awake spiritually. I started to search; I had a desire to know God. I had always believed there was a God, but now I wanted to know him personally.

As my spiritual sensitivity became sharper, I began to write poetry to express the understandings I was gleaning. The reality of God had lain dormant in my life for more than a dozen years, but now I was awakened to try to find and make my own that which my heart spurred me to seek.

I suddenly became inspired to attempt to share my heart-thoughts in verse; this went on for eight months. Two

---

[4] This term is used in some countries, such as the United States, to refer to a person who has experienced the baptism of the Holy Spirit (as understood in the Charismatic Renewal).

months later I told a friend that I wanted a Bible, and he made me a present of a King James Version Bible covered in white leather. Inside the Bible's front cover he wrote this inscription, 'Kim, this is the road map that leads to Eternity . . .' He urged me to begin by reading 1 Corinthians 13, Paul's chapter on agapé love—and to learn it well.

By July of that year I had made progress and, from what I can tell now, was on the verge of finding Jesus and surrendering my life to him. Somehow, however, I did not find the road that the Lord was showing me, though I was obviously quite close to it. I again strayed from the rays of God's saving grace and wandered down many false paths that led to dead ends, trying to learn what life was about. It was to take me eight more turbulent years before I celebrated my homecoming to the Lord.

My heart had become keenly aware that July that I had a mission to fulfil in life, but I did not know it was for God. All my inner feelings about this told me that I would be working with the multitudes, helping them to help themselves.

My career at this point was progressing very rapidly and I came under mounting pressures from my workload and from international travel. I went through a period during which I experienced extreme fatigue. A doctor diagnosed my condition as complete physical exhaustion, put me in hospital for a few days, and prescribed librium, a mood stabiliser, saying the drug might help me regain some balance. I hesitated about actually beginning therapy with this drug. I regarded any reliance on this kind of medicine as a crutch, an admission of weakness. But one day a close friend persuaded me to follow the doctor's advice. I started to take the librium each day.

The year 1971 started off fine: everything in my career looked positive and smooth. I was now part of an international team of five—four men and myself—which had responsibilities in the company for overseeing all our foreign subsidiaries. I made plans for my children to join me in Florida once their current school year ended.

Towards the end of January I was in the midst of preparing for my first business trip to Europe to see executives of the corporation's subsidiaries in England, Switzerland, Italy and Greece. I rang my mother to check on my sons and share with her my excitement about the trip. She seemed fine. What I could not know was that before that week was out she would go home to the Lord. On Thursday, while I was in Zurich, I received a call from my father late at night, saying that she had suddenly fallen critically ill. She had been rushed to the hospital, then had gone into a coma. Doctors could not determine what was wrong.

I flew home as soon as I could, arriving in Mansfield at 1.0 am. Dad and I decided to go to see mother in the hospital at 7.0 am. But at 3.0 am a neighbour knocked on our door. She said the hospital had called her because we had not heard our phone ring and it was her painful duty to inform us that my mother had just died. She was sixty-three years old.

After the funeral, as I was preparing to go back to Florida, Dad asked me if I would allow the children to continue to live with him; he did not want to be alone. Within two weeks, however, he called me and said handling the children was then too much for him and could I please come and get them?

Things were going to be changing again.

Immediately, I had to prepare to receive my boys. I bought a large four-bedroom Polynesian-style home with a beautiful lawn, shrubbery and a swimming pool, located in an exclusive area of Altamonte Springs near Orlando. A wonderful Catholic woman of Portuguese descent came to live with us to help me look after the boys for the next five years. Periodically, my father came to stay with us for several months at a time.

Then Dad sold our family home in Ohio and moved to a Florida town near the St John's River, only two and a half hours away from us. Often he came to our house for a week or so stay; sometimes the boys would go and stay with him.

Finally my children and I were back together as a family.

The boys seemed to adjust well to their new life, quickly making friends and getting into sports. Darin became friends with a neighbouring Greek boy and occasionally went with him to the Greek Orthodox church. Robert was accepted into a private naval academy in St Petersburg, Florida, where he would live and study for several years, coming home just for vacations.

On the career front there were changes to come. International travel intensified as I undertook trips to Hong Kong, Korea, and Australia, as well as continuing with travel to Europe. Later that spring I was made a director of the corporation's international holding company, again as the only woman. Then came an even more dramatic development: the international team I was part of decided to leave the company that autumn and to form our own international management and marketing consultancy firm. We could continue to serve our previous employer under a consulting contract, but we would be free to serve other clients and to create new companies. We then took the new firm public on the Montreal stock exchange. My business future seemed assured.

3

Becoming freer

On the outside things looked good; but all was not well. For one thing I felt very restless, and I could not pin down why. In 1973 Patti came to Orlando to visit me and renew our friendship. She arrived with her little son from Texas, where she had moved after marriage, to stay with us for a week. As soon as she saw me, she realised something was wrong. Very quickly she picked up that I had been relying on librium to cast off the pressures from my life.

For three years I had continued to take this drug, particularly whenever I found myself a bit depressed or having trouble coping with my free time. I had only recently come to understand that the drug was gaining a strong hold over me.

'Why don't you just stop taking that?' Patti asked me.

'I've come to the same conclusion,' I told her, 'only I feel I should wait until my current work crisis subsides—then I'll stop. I promise.'

Only years later did I find out that, as I slept that week, Patti, God's number one prayer warrior on my behalf, had been on her knees in her bedroom, praying to the Lord to break my reliance on librium.

Later that week Patti asked me again, 'Kim, why don't you quit taking those capsules?'

This time something clicked inside me. I found myself saying aloud, 'Yes? Why not? I believe I will.' And from that moment on I never took another. Years later I would praise God mightily for the way he set me free that night.

Several months later, however, I ran into another obstacle on my path. An acquaintance gave me a book called *The Seth Material* by Jane Roberts. The material was said to have been dictated by an 'entity' called 'Seth' through Jane Roberts while she was in a semi-trance, her husband taking down what the 'entity' supposedly was saying through her.

Unfortunately, this material had a large enough framework to include virtually all the spiritual beliefs I had come into contact with, including a distorted version of Christianity. The reading of this book, and others by the same author, over the next several years, etched deeper and deeper into my soul a completely false set of beliefs.

In spring 1974 I made a major business decision. I decided to launch my own management and marketing consulting firm. I soon received a substantial contract from a multinational firm to create a company to distribute and market hydro-culture plants. With the help of staff from that company I carried out test marketing for these products in 1975. After the market test proved successful, my firm received a contract to develop a new corporation to market the hydro-culture plant-growing system. This involved generating distribution centres and creating a sales network.

This marketing project was almost like a child to me, since I had been a part of its conception and nurtured it through the various stages of its development. At the end of our first year, we had locations in eight states and had achieved retail sales of over one million dollars. Then, suddenly, because of a situation totally beyond my control, my contract was unjustly cancelled. In one day my 'child' had been taken away from me. This loss was very painful—I had put so much of myself into the project.

After this setback I decided to take time away from my career. I thought I would take at least a year off. I wanted to spend more time with my boys, now aged fourteen and ten, and take care of my home. My self-imposed sabbatical, however, would last longer than I had planned. It went on for two and a half years.

In this period, however, I did agree to serve on the board of directors of a television station serving the Orlando area. At one point the Christian Broadcasting Network (CBN) from Virginia Beach sent three men to discuss buying the station. Though the negotiations ended inconclusively I found myself impressed by the way these men conducted themselves in business—with calmness, politeness, honesty and integrity. They seemed far removed from the common worldly ways of many business people I had known. This set me to thinking about the differences I had perceived between committed Christians and non-believers.

4

Nine months to new life

During my sabbatical I continued to project an aura of success, as I had sufficient resources, an attractive home and an outgoing, positive manner. Inside however I was growing more and more restless. There had to be, I told myself, more than worldly success, financial security, and prestige. My heart was even then crying out for my Lord—but I didn't realise it.

In the middle of this period, in September 1977, on the last day of my thirty-third year, I was trimming my lawn and garden when I felt a renewed call and a new openness to the spiritual dimension such as I had not experienced since 1970. I felt a determination in my heart to pursue that 'knowing' within that told me I had a mission in life and not to stop until I understood what it was. Thus began the last nine months that brought me home to Jesus.

When that last phase of my journey began, all my spiritual beliefs were false. I believed that Jesus was a great teacher, a master, a prophet, but that there were others like him; I did not recognise him as the Son of God, my Saviour and Redeemer. I believed that somehow all the world's religions blended together to form a great global oneness. I believed that 'Satan' was not a real being, just a term that some people used to describe evil.

As I pored over what was in my heart, I became keenly aware that my spiritual beliefs at that time were like paper walls, and that they were starting to crumble. I had been counselling a group of young people who came to my house periodically to talk about various spiritual perspectives, and I had led them into many of my own beliefs (which I would soon find out had been false). Suddenly I felt I had to tell them to stop coming to see me for a while. My spiritual understandings were changing so fast I was totally unsure of what to convey to them and what to hold back, or modify.

My spirit cried out to the Spirit of Truth to bring me, at long last, into the light. And there is only *one* Spirit of Truth—the Holy Spirit! In those nine months I accomplished an incredible journey, the intensity of which outdid anything I had experienced before.

During this time everything in my life began to fall apart. I had heart-crushing difficulties with my children. My older son, Robert, then sixteen, had four car accidents within four months, got injured in football and had to quit that sport, and then had serious problems in school. His younger brother, Darin, got into trouble with school and juvenile authorities three times. I became ill with a series of kidney infections. My teeth gave me trouble and I had to have dental surgery. It just seemed that everything negative that could happen was actually happening, all at once. Emotionally, I felt worn down.

Churning inside me was the question, 'When is it ever going to stop?'

I tried to put into practice all the positive thinking techniques I had ever heard of, but they didn't work. The feeling of being caught up in a cataclysm kept up unabated.

I felt, in fact, that I was running a race, that I *had* to get to a certain place at a certain time. But I still did not know where that place was—or just when I was due to arrive there. What I could not have realised at that point was that a battle was being waged for my spirit, a battle between Satan and the Lord. I came to see later that God had had an appointed hour for my mission to begin, and that that hour fell in the year 1980. In order for me to be launched into my role in God's plan I had to be home to him in a hurry—for it was then 1978.

The last two months of this journey were the toughest of all. Suddenly, I came in contact with Christians seemingly in tandem with persons representing other beliefs (just as had happened in 1969). My corporation was approached for a possible contract by another firm that dealt with hydroculture plants and cosmetics. This company had a born-again Christian[5] as president and a vice-president who was a psychic and involved in eastern philosophies. In another group I was dealing with, a Christian executive and his wife had a business association with a woman who had strong

---

[5] A term commonly used in evangelical and Pentecostal circles to designate persons who have made a heart commitment to accept Jesus as Lord and Saviour of their lives. See John 3.3–8.

metaphysical beliefs. In this period too the Mormons began to visit me at home every week, and I explored with them the Mormon religion.

By far the most dramatic contact I had came with the world of the occult. This began when I unexpectedly came across a young woman, a secretary, whom I had known from work in 1972. She told me her life had greatly changed, that she had acquired 'psychic abilities'. Her gift, she said, was 'psychometry', or the ability to hold an object and then tell from its 'vibrations' all about its owner's past and future. She said she had been studied by a university's parapsychology department. Researchers used objects from ancient civilisations and she would hold them and tell all about the civilisations, scoring, she said, very high on all tests. When I asked her what she was now doing, she replied that she had developed this 'mediumistic' talent into a nightclub act. She worked at a club in Orlando, taking objects from customers and telling them their past and future.

One day she came to visit me at my home and asked me if I would like to go with her to a psychic convention in Miami. Because of the intensity of my spiritual search, I agreed to go. When we arrived at the convention, where about a thousand people were gathered, I felt very strange. It was as if something was wrong. However, I could not tell what. Then inwardly I perceived running through my thoughts these words: 'This is not for you. There is something else.' The convention had brought together spiritualists, mediums, astrologers, white witches, palm readers, tarot card readers and psychics, as well as their followers. There were seminars on pyramid energy, UFOs, white witchcraft, Kundilini and Hatha yoga, transcendental meditation, psychic healing and more. As we mingled with the participants I remarked to myself, 'These people seem very nice. They aren't at all weird in dress or manner.' Again, however, I perceived the words, 'This is not for you. There is something else.'

I was so relieved when we left and glad when I arrived home—though I still could not explain to myself why I had been so uncomfortable at the convention.

Between the positive thinking, eastern philosophies, the Mormons, and the occult, plus my own fierce and unsatisfied inner urge to find my mission in life, I felt I was being pushed to the limit. At one point in this period I felt an inner urge to get my Bible down off a shelf and out of a box it had sat in almost since it had been presented to me as a gift on Mother's Day, 1970.

I began by reading Revelation. What seemed to be impressed upon my thoughts was that Revelation had secret meanings, yet undeciphered—that actually everything in the book was meant to be understood as opposite to what was literally being said. (Obviously, I did not yet know Satan's wiles and deceptions, nor did I have any idea of how hard he was trying to keep me from finding the truth.)

With all the pressures bearing upon me I decided I had to get away. I made a spontaneous decision to book a flight to California and spend a week there alone. The first place I visited was Death Valley, where I spent three days in the national park and climbed to the highest point in the area, a place called Dante's View. While I sat there looking out over Death Valley, a desolate, cactus-pocked desert, the thought came to me, 'Look where you are; this is where most people would say death is, but truly, this is where life is.' I suddenly felt a calm around that I had not experienced in months. This sense of tranquility appeared to me to confirm the impressions I had had earlier about Revelation needing to be interpreted as opposite to what was written. How deceived I was! Because those thoughts and that calm, I could see later, were *not* from the Lord.

I returned to Florida still feeling pushed to the absolute limit. Each day in these last two months seemed like a whole year. During my eight-year pilgrimage toward the truth I had learned how to be open, how to be led, how to follow. The only trouble, as I was soon to understand, was that spiritual warfare was being waged between the Holy Spirit and Satan. The confusion was wrenching.

On Saturday evening, June 10, 1978, I made a telephone call to a Baptist minister and his Pentecostal wife, a couple with whom I had been discussing a business venture. I asked if I could come to their house the next day, earlier than the time already scheduled for a business meeting. 'I want to talk to you about spiritual matters,' I said.

When I got there I began to tell them what I had been going through; however, neither of them seemed able to comprehend my spiritual struggles very well, or to offer me any immediate answers. Others arrived and we had our business meeting. When that was over I said to the wife, 'I don't feel as if I'm supposed to leave.'

That really appeared to startle her. 'Well,' she said after she had collected her thoughts, 'would you like to come to church with us tonight?'

Unhesitatingly, I accepted their invitation. They gave me the address of the church, a place called the Charismatic Teaching Centre, and I went home and changed my clothes to get ready to go there.

I had been keeping highlights of my spiritual journey in an appointment calendar that had only days of the week printed on its pages. I grabbed this little black calendar book and my Bible, and left.

When I reached the church I sat down and flipped to the date of that day, which was June 11, written on the bottom section of a right-hand page. For some reason I flipped to the next page, where it should have been marked 'June 12', but there were no more dates written in. Three weeks previously I had written in all the dates up until June 11 and stopped there.

It struck me in that instant that I had found what I had been looking for. My journey—ragged, twisting and painful as it had been—was over; it would end here, in the place where I now sat; it would end here, on this night . . . June 11, 1978.

II
CALL TO MINISTRY

CALL TO MINISTRY

The pastor of the Charismatic Teaching Centre appeared and began the service. These people had a type of joyous praise and worship that I was totally unfamiliar with: praying spontaneously out loud, hands raised with palms upwards or else clapping.

That evening, unlike the many Sundays at the little Baptist church near my house in Mansfield, Ohio, where my timidity and reticence had won out, I went forward (even before anyone gave an invitation to do so), stood in front of the assembly and publicly gave my life to Jesus. 'Lord,' I prayed, 'use me, do anything with me. I'm yours.'

When the pastor issued an invitation to 'anyone who would like to receive the Baptism in the Holy Spirit,'[6] my hand flew up almost before I knew what it was doing. Then the pastor said, 'as evidenced by speaking in tongues,' and my first thought was, 'What if I don't get it?' God, however,

---

[6] As Fr Francis A. Sullivan, SJ, has written: 'Classical Pentecostals and Protestant neo-Pentecostals generally use this phrase to indicate a second blessing posterior to conversion, a new imparting of the Spirit. When Romans Catholics use the phrase it usually means the breaking forth into conscious experience of the Spirit who was given during the celebration of initiation (baptism).' *Charisms and Charismatic Renewal*, p63, Servant Books, Ann Arbor, Michigan.

was mightier than my fears. My spirit was enveloped in God's love. I didn't even know what this 'baptism' consisted of, but if it was from God, I wanted everything that he had for me.

As people laid hands upon me and prayed that God would fill me with his Holy Spirit, a new way of expressing my love for God welled up in me and issued forth from my lips. My tongue was forming new sounds, and I found myself praying in a 'language' other than English.

After Jesus baptised me in his Holy Spirit, the pastor prophesied over me. I did not know what the gift of prophecy was about; everything was new to me in the charismatic dimension. But as he spoke in prophecy that the Lord God had a calling on, or mission for, my life, that he intended to use me in his service, my spirit leapt within me.

'See?' it felt my spirit was exclaiming to me, 'I told you so! I told you so!'

God had stirred that calling for eight years. And I realised on that night in Orlando, Florida, the deep truth of the scripture, 'It is not you that have chosen me; it is I who have chosen you' (John 15.16). For eight years I had felt the impact of that call upon my heart, but for so long I had been so lost that I didn't even know it was the Lord. I praised him for his patience and his persistence in seeking me out and drawing me back to him like the prodigal son.

As the prophetic word was spoken over me that night it also promised that the journey I would make with the Lord would not be easy. In my heart I thought, 'Nothing could be harder than my past nine months of trying to find you, Lord.' But I was to learn that the cost of discipleship to Jesus is high. Often there would be pain, and often tears. In surrendering ourselves and our desires to the Lord we pledge to take up our cross and follow him—and be crucified with him.[7]

---

[7] See Luke 9.23.

5

Triumph over evil

After the service some of us went out for coffee. One woman in the group, a missionary who had just returned from a time in Israel, had a book about areas of spiritual darkness. Knowing that I would need to learn quickly about spiritual warfare, she made me a present of it.

The Pentecostal woman who, with her Baptist husband, had brought me to the church, also gave me some parting advice that evening as we said farewell: 'Forget the past,' she said. 'Because you sought forgiveness of your sins tonight, your sins have been washed away by Jesus' blood. Stay in his Word, because God needs to teach you and feed you and establish his Word in your heart. Finally, keep praying in tongues, in the new prayer language the Lord has given you.'

That was the first time I had realised that this language I had prayed in was something I could evoke on my own. Driving home, I opened my mouth to pray and it was wonderful to hear that heavenly language pour out. Late into the night I continued to express gratitude to God using the new tongue he had given me.

When I arrived at my house both my sons were in bed and asleep. Even though I was excited about sharing with them my rediscovery of the Lord, I decided I would have to wait till morning. I went into my bedroom, sat down on the bed, and began to go through the book on areas of spiritual darkness. Now my perception was totally different. In a flash I could clearly see many of the errors of my previous beliefs and exactly how I had been deceived. For instance, I saw how I had walked into Satan's den by attending the psychic convention in Miami. Coming across warnings in Deuteronomy 18.10–12 and Isaiah 47.13–14 I could see how they applied to many of the convention's activities. The verses from Deuteronomy read: 'Let no one be found among you who sacrifices his own son or daughter in the fire, who practises divination or sorcery, interprets omens, engages in witchcraft or casts spells, or who is a medium or spiritist or who consults the dead. Anyone who does these things is detestable to the Lord.' And the verses from Isaiah read: 'All the counsel you have received has only worn you out! Let your astrologers come forward, those stargazers who make predictions month by month, let them save you from what is coming upon you. Surely they are like stubble; the fire will burn them up. They cannot even save themselves from the power of the flame.'

I decided I would destroy all the books that had instilled in me so many false beliefs, that had kept me from finding Jesus. These were books that I had gathered along my way over the previous eight years. And I did destroy them, I burned them. I did not want those books to fall into others' hands and create deception the way they had for me. From that point onwards I wanted only the things of the Lord in my home. How grateful I was for the greatness of my Lord's mercy and his never-ending forgiving love.

The next morning, when my sons got up for breakfast, I was still overflowing with joy and wanted to share with them immediately everything that I had lived the evening before. I told them that I had met Jesus that night in his full love and power.

They looked at me rather strangely, because I had never even taken my children to church. I had come to the 'reasonable' decision that I would let them make up their own minds about God and church 'when they were old enough'. Robert had, several years prior to my conversion, actually broached the subject of God with me. I could not respond to his questions, however, because I did not know the answers then myself. He subsequently came to the conclusion that God did not exist. His mother, supposedly his prime spiritual counsellor, had let him wander onto that train of thought by being so mute.

'O Lord,' I cried out that day, 'what have I done to my children?'

Later in the afternoon, I met with the woman missionary I

had been introduced to the night before and related my concern about my sons. She showed me Acts 16.31, 'Believe in the Lord Jesus and you will be saved—you and your household.' Something came alive in my heart, knowing that what I desired, the salvation of my children, God desired too, and that through faith in his promises, it was already accomplished.

What I could not realise then was that one day in the not too distant future God would call me to leave my children as he would move me across an ocean and plant me in foreign soil. There were many sacrifices ahead; in fact, I probably would have trembled had I known of them at the outset. What I have learned is that God always gives the grace to take each step that he calls you to take as you arrive at that step. Even though sometimes you become aware of the grace only *after* you have taken the step. All I knew then was that I loved my Lord, that I was truly sorry I had been stuck in the brambles of sin and darkness so long, that I wanted to fulfil his commission for my life.

As I continued my talk with the missionary, she began to teach me about the power of Jesus' blood,[8] and of Jesus' name—how his name was greater than any other,[9] how he had already triumphed over evil, over every demonic force.[10]

She said that I would probably have many bouts of spiritual warfare and that I needed to understand what it was 'to put on the whole armour of God'. We opened our Bibles and turned together to Ephesians 6, where she began to read aloud:

'Finally, my brethren, be strong in the Lord, and in the power of his might. Put on the whole armour of God, that ye may be able to stand against the wiles of the devil. For we wrestle not against flesh and blood, but against principalities, against powers, against the rulers of darkness of this world, against spiritual wickedness in high places.

---

[8] See Ephesians 1.7.   [9] See Philippians 2.9–11.   [10] See Colossians 2.15.

'Wherefore take unto you the whole armour of God, that ye may be able to withstand in the evil day, and having done all, to stand' (Ephesians 6.10–13, KJV).

She wanted me to understand that there definitely *was* an enemy—Satan and his demons, fallen angels—and that God had equipped me to go forth against that enemy in God's own armour.

As she taught me about each part of the armour I began to enter into an understanding of who I was in Jesus Christ, and of the fact that I could do nothing in my own power but all things would be accomplished through the power of his Holy Spirit. 'Not by might, not by power, but by my Spirit, saith the Lord of Hosts.' (Zechariah 4.6, KJV).

During the third night after my conversion I went through an experience that I felt was like a satanic encounter. Whether it was with Satan himself or with his demonic forces I do not know. Apparently I had been asleep for a short time; something happened and it seemed that I awoke; however, I was not actually awake; I was not dreaming; I do not know what state I was in. The atmosphere felt dark and evil, and I could not escape. In that state I lived through three dramatic scenes.

In the first scene the sliding glass doors of my bedroom leading out to the patio suddenly became a screen. A power that I recognised as demonic manifested itself in the guise of one of my dogs and came at me gnashing his teeth, snarling ferociously, but he couldn't get to me; the screen hindered him. I had an inner awareness that Satan had been defeated by the blood of the Lamb and I had nothing to fear. I began to call out boldly, 'Jesus . . . ! Jesus . . . !' Finally, that image broke.

Then came scene two: The demonic power manifested itself in the form of a young man that I knew. We were in a car driving at high speed. Suddenly he was trying to push me out the door. Again, as I spoke the name 'Jesus!' this image broke, even more quickly than the first.

Only to give place to a third scene: I found myself in the back yard with my three dogs, my two sons and some neighbouring children. The children were in the midst of play. All at once the demonic power took the form of a white Alaskan husky which came up and started to fight with my sheepdog. It was a bloody fight and my dog was injured and bleeding. I picked him up to carry him into my room. As I entered through the sliding glass doors, his foot dropped off. A great anger mounted in me; I rose up and invoked the power of the blood of Jesus—and broke out of whatever state I was in, knowing that 'greater is he that is in you, than he that is in the world' (1 John 4.4, KJV).

Over the next few weeks I spent many hours with the missionary woman learning from her about Jesus and his ways. I also learned about the Holy Spirit, and about his gifts and his fruit. Together we studied 1 Corinthians 12: 'Now concerning spiritual gifts, brethren, I would not have you ignorant . . .'

'Always remember,' she told me, 'that the gifts are, as it says in Ephesians 4.12: "to prepare God's people for works of service so that the Body of Christ may be built up". They are not given primarily for the individual Christian, but for the good of the whole Body.'

This woman also taught me how important it was to be open to the working of the Holy Spirit in my life. To live in the Spirit, to walk in the Spirit and to be led of the Spirit;[11] not to quench the Spirit[12] nor to grieve the Spirit.[13] She also counselled me to learn about the gifts of the Holy Spirit and their different manifestations.

At that time the only gift of which I had first-hand knowledge was the gift of tongues which I used in prayer and praise. The gift of tongues, in its use for individual prayer, is probably the most commonly distributed gift of the Holy Spirit in the Body of Christ today, and often the first one received.

Through my discussions with the missionary I also learned that when I did not know how to pray for something,

---

[11] See Galatians 5.18, 25.   [12] See 1 Thessalonians 5.19.   [13] See Ephesians 4.30a.

I could pray by simply speaking out the need and then praying with the gift of tongues, as Paul teaches in Romans 8.26–27. During my first year 'in the Lord' I used this gift continuously to pray for everything. I was just beginning to grow in my knowledge of God's Word and his ways and I did not yet know how to pray properly with my understanding.

I was taught not to seek after the gifts first, but rather to seek the Giver, and especially to allow the Lord to develop in me the *fruit* of the Spirit. This, as described by Paul, is 'love, joy, peace, patience, kindness, goodness, faithfulness, gentleness and self-control' (Galatians 5.22–23, RSV).

I recalled then the friend's advice in 1970 to begin reading the Bible he had given me with 1 Corinthians 13, and to learn that chapter well. 'Everything,' he had told me, 'should flow forth from love, the love that comes from God.' Rereading the chapter now I could understand what he meant. This rereading created a strong desire in my heart to have God's love spring alive in me and turn me into an instrument of that love—in everything that I did.

6

'. . . I am God'

The Sunday after my coming home to the Lord, ten minutes before I was to leave the house for evening services my son Darin, fresh from a heated argument with his brother, smashed his hand against his chest of drawers to vent his anger. He came out of his room and said, 'Mom, I think I just broke my hand. And I need you to take me to the hospital.'

I inspected his hand; it was very swollen; it appeared that the bone on the third knuckle of his hand had been broken but had not pierced the skin. Or possibly it had been severely dislocated. Darin at first was in great pain and then his hand went numb.

Dressed only in gym shorts and a T-shirt and not wearing any shoes, Darin got into the car and we headed off toward the hospital. On the way these words kept resounding in my heart, 'Jesus heals . . . ! Jesus heals . . . !' I felt the Holy Spirit was challenging me to reach out to the Lord for the healing of my son before I took him to the hospital.

As I approached an intersection I knew that if I went straight across and continued my direction I would soon be at the hospital emergency room. If I turned left I would soon be at the church. I had to stop for a red light. I made the decision to take Darin, who was then twelve years old, first to the Lord. As the light changed to green I turned left and started to drive toward the church.

'Mom!' Darin exclaimed, '*what* are you doing? *Where* are you going?' He knew the way to the hospital only too well because of other boyhood accidents he had had.

'We're going first to church to ask the Lord to heal your hand,' I said. He sat there bewildered, not saying anything more. By this point his arm had gone numb up to his elbow.

When I arrived at the church the service had already begun. I found an usher and told him about Darin's condition and asked him to locate the two women whom I was to meet there and invite them to come outside. Darin stayed in the car. Soon the usher and the two women appeared and we went to Darin and, all standing with him outside the car, began to pray. The other three laid hands on Darin, and so did I. Aloud they prayed for God's healing love to enter his hand and heal it. Then they prayed in tongues and I joined them.

Throughout this whole episode I kept my eyes tightly closed, thinking that perhaps if I were to look, I'd begin to doubt. When I finally dared open my eyes, I was amazed at what I saw: the swelling and redness in Darin's hand appeared to have vanished; the bone that had either been broken or dislocated had moved back into place. Feeling had returned to Darin's arm and he could move his hand and arm freely.

One woman asked him if he would like to come into the church and thank the Lord for what had happened. He said 'yes'. So there he was in church, the first time he had ever been there with me, in bare feet, gym shorts and T-shirt. We stayed through the service. Afterwards somebody suggested that we have his hand X-rayed and otherwise checked.

I asked Darin what he wanted to do.

'If you don't mind, Mom, let's go to the hospital,' he said. Then he added, 'Mom, do you know why I went into that church with you? The only reason was because I didn't want to embarrass you.' I thought to myself, 'The Lord sure has funny ways.'

At the hospital we had X-rays taken. The results came back negative: nothing broken, nothing dislocated. Everything was in order.

The next morning, however, Darin came into my bedroom and told me he was feeling pain in his hand. I put my hand gently on his and prayed for him in the manner I had learned the previous day at church. I asked Jesus to banish the pain. Then I went to the kitchen to make my son some breakfast. When I returned, bringing him the food I had prepared, he exclaimed, 'Mom, all the pain is gone!' That afternoon Darin even went roller-skating. The pain never returned. In the episode of the healing of Darin's hand and in other ways, as this new Christian life unfolded, my Father in heaven surprised me with signs of his love.

On Sunday evening, June 25, as the service began, I opened my King James Version Bible at random and my eyes fell on passages of Isaiah which were underlined in purple ink. How, I asked myself, had *that* happened? I hadn't done the underlining, and the Bible was brand new. No matter, the message of the underscored passages spoke very strongly to my heart:

From Isaiah 41:

10: 'Fear thou not; for I am with thee: Be not dismayed; for I am thy God: I will strengthen thee; yea, I will help thee; yea, I will uphold thee with the right hand of my righteousness.'

13: 'For I the Lord thy God will hold thy right hand, saying unto thee, Fear not; I will help thee.'

From Isaiah 43:

2: 'When thou passest through the waters, I will be with thee . . .'

3: 'For I am the Lord thy God . . .'

5: 'Fear not: for I am with thee . . .'

10: 'Ye are my witnesses, saith the Lord, and my servant whom I have chosen: that ye may know and believe me . . .'

11: 'I, even I, am the Lord; and besides me there is no saviour.'

12: '. . . I am God.'

As these lines pierced my innermost being I was so overwhelmed that I could not follow the rest of the service. These words from the Lord were exactly what I had needed. To this day they continue to encourage my spirit, especially in times of trial, assuring me that the Lord is always with us.

Since I had no recollection at that point that I had been baptised as a child, I decided I should receive baptism by water. On a sunny afternoon my missionary friend immersed me in a pool of water and baptised me 'in the name of the Father, the Son and the Holy Spirit'.

There was an element of 'unfinished business'—the group of young people with whom I had been sharing my beliefs about a year before and whom I had asked to stop coming to my house. Shortly after my conversion I went to visit each of them and to tell them what I had found, that, exactly as John 14.6 says, Jesus is 'the Way and the Truth and the Life' and no one comes to the Father except through him. On Sunday morning, July 1, I invited them to meet me at my house, and along with my Dad and my two sons, eight of us in all, we went to church together.

After the service Robert left as quickly as he could. All the others stayed to pray. Darin accepted Jesus as his Lord for the first time, and the other young people and my Dad rededicated their lives to the Lord. My Dad was seventy-eight at the time. All received prayer for the baptism of the

Holy Spirit and all went home that day praising God in a new language, the gift of tongues.

I also went to share with the secretary-turned-psychic. However, she was not open to receive my experiences with the Lord. My words fell on ears deaf to this life-giving message. This woman's whole life now revolved around her 'mediumistic' talent, and she was not ready, or willing, to renounce her practices as wrong and not of God. All I could do for her after that was to continue to carry her in my prayers, asking that the revelation light of the Holy Spirit would pierce the darkness that surrounded her.

Three weeks after my conversion, on a farm in North Carolina, I found myself sharing with a friend about my experience with Jesus. As the joy of the Lord was so strong inside me I probably was a bit overpowering. During my sharing about what Jesus had done for Darin and me, the twelve-year-old son of this friend listened intently. He said he believed in Jesus but had never been baptised. Later that day he and my son Darin came to me and asked if they could be baptised. So we had a double baptism in the creek that day.

Then the friend I was visiting told me, 'There's going to be a prayer meeting here on Thursday with people who have become charismatic like you, if you'd like to go.' I didn't need much persuasion. At that meeting the speaker was a Jamaican-American woman named Rosali Edwards. As she shared her own experiences of Jesus, she told us that she and her husband had been called by God to build a retreat and conference centre for the Lord, named 'Beulah', located in the rugged back country of central North Carolina. Their big annual July barbecue and praise celebration would be held two days hence, she said, and all of us were invited to come. I felt an impression on my heart that I should go. Two days later I set off to find Beulah, which they explained to me meant 'the land in which God delights'.[14]

---

[14] See Isaiah 62.4.

The Beulah Retreat and Conference Centre lies twenty-five miles south of Chapel Hill in scrubby pine forests reached by dusty back roads. It's about a three and half hour drive from the farm. While I was driving to Beulah, God somehow communicated to me the first geographical move on my journey in his Spirit. I didn't know how or why I suddenly realised that I was to move myself and my family to Dallas, Texas, but I just knew. I also had a notion of 'two years' . . . but I didn't then know what that meant.

That day at Beulah, in the midst of glorious praise and worship among mostly black brothers and sisters, I felt a confirmation about the move. Even as I was approaching the day of my conversion, I had begun to sense that a move lay ahead, possibly to California, possibly to Texas. It was, it seems, the Spirit readying the terrain in my heart to accept the decision.

At Beulah that afternoon we took communion together. This was my first communion since my return to the Lord. It drew me into a special union with Jesus that I hadn't experienced in any other way.

7

Dallas

Shortly after that, on a Thursday morning, I took a plane trip to Texas to look around and see if God would confirm the move further. I had business contacts in that state, and my sister-in-law and her husband lived in Dallas. A business acquaintance arranged for me to have the use of her apartment while she was away.

The day after I arrived in Dallas and picked up a rental car I began to look for housing for myself and my sons. By that afternoon I had become feverish with a cold and a kidney infection. I was so sick that I went to a hospital emergency room for treatment, then went to my lodging and spent the next two days in bed. I was alone and weak in a large city, and desperate to find somebody to have Christian fellowship with. I looked in the phone book for a church where I could attend a Sunday service. The only word I knew was 'charismatic'. I found only one church listing with that word in it and quickly called the church; it was rebuilding and was temporarily not open to visitors.

By Sunday evening I was feeling quite low and thought my whole exploratory trip to Dallas was very likely a mistake. I said to myself, 'I didn't really hear God telling me to move to Dallas; God doesn't really want me out here.' I made plans to fly home to Orlando on Monday.

All I had had was enough faith to last for four days. Later, reflecting back on this experience, I would begin to understand what Jesus meant when he said to his disciples, 'O ye of little faith!'

Close to what I thought was my plane time I phoned my sister-in-law's husband, telling him I would not be able to visit as planned because I had decided to fly home right away. He asked me what time my plane was to leave and I told him. 'Well,' came his voice over the line, 'you've already missed your plane.' My watch had stopped, and the plane to Orlando had gone.

So I made plans to go home the next day, staying another night in the apartment. Everything was set: I had plenty of time to drive to the airport, return my rental car and catch my flight. But I drove in the wrong direction. When I realised my mistake I was about sixty miles from the airport and knew I would miss my plane again. All I could feel around me was confusion.

'This is just too much,' I said to myself. 'I am going to stop and get quiet and wait on the Lord. I'm not going anywhere until I find out what *he* wants and not what *I* want.' So I decided to stop trying to go back to Orlando until I could see more clearly.

I went to my sister-in-law's house and told her and her husband what had happened to me, also sharing with them my recent conversion experience. The next day they put me in touch with two local Christian businessmen who had also experienced the baptism in the Holy Spirit and I finally found the fellowship I had been looking for. During this stay in Dallas, which lasted three weeks, I also received an assurance in my heart that this indeed was the city where God wanted me to live.

One challenge created by my impending move was financial. I did not then have the resources to make the move, and I said, 'Lord, if this move to Dallas is your will, you also have the money I need to carry it out.' Within two days after my return to Orlando I received notice that a long overdue debt would be paid; the money was more than enough to cover the move. That was the final confirmation.

My two sons protested that the move sounded illogical. I vetoed their objections, telling them only that I felt that this was how the Holy Spirit was leading us. Within three weeks we had loaded up a large houseful of furniture into a removal van, and in two cars packed with two growing boys and three dogs, we moved 1,500 miles in faith.

I had already rented a place for us to settle in the Dallas area, in Rockwall, a town of seven thousand people, situated on a large man-made reservoir, Lake Ray Hubbard. My sons were mollified by what they saw: our home was right on the lakefront in a complex that had a swimming pool, tennis courts, and a nine-hole golf-course. When we got to the townhouse I had chosen and carried everything in, I said to God, 'Lord, here I am. All the instructions I had from you were just to move here. You'll have to show me what to do next.' I had so much zeal to do the work of the Lord, and no common sense.

The first week wasn't bad because I was busy unpacking. I found in the city of Farmers Branch, Texas, a church in which to worship which was interdenominational and charismatic.

By the end of the second week, though, I had most of the

unpacking done and still no idea what I would be doing in Dallas. A third week went by. Abraham of course waited twenty-five years before *he* saw the fulfilment of God's promise, but during my short but seemingly interminable wait, I did not yet know that story about Abraham. Four weeks went by, then five . . .

In the sixth week something happened. The phone rang and a man introduced himself and said that he had a corporation in Dallas and had been given my name by a business contact in Orlando.

The man asked me if I would be interested in taking on a new business project; it turned out to be a project identical to one my management and marketing consulting firm had carried out in 1976—creating a marketing plan and a company for the sale of hydroculture plants. I made an appointment to see this businessman, but my heart wasn't in it. I had no desire to enter business again.

After my meeting with him I sought the Lord: 'What is your way, O God? What do *you* want?'

Though a plunge into a new consulting contract had not been my personal desire, I felt, after I had prayed, that the Lord was inclining me to accept the offer. It was exactly such a contract to create and develop a sales company in Florida that I had lost in 1976 through no fault of my own. It seemed to me that what had been taken away was being restored, even if it would only be for a time.

'If this is your place for me, Lord,' I said, 'I ask just one thing: that you allow me the liberty to direct a company for your glory, for your honour; that you allow me not only to teach spiritual motivational principles, but also to proclaim that *only under the lordship of Jesus* should these principles be exercised.'

Before my conversion, when I was first exposed to 'positive thinking' material, I had not understood what this material was all about. I knew that exponents of positive thinking even linked some of their principles to the Bible, comparing, for example, the Scripture 'as man thinks in his heart, so is he' (see Proverbs 23.7) with the purely secular principle, 'Whatever the mind can conceive of and believe in, it can achieve.' Now I could clearly see the dangers implicit in such material. Secular positive thinking techniques frequently draw one into an 'I' dimension: 'I' can do anything —or everything. The techniques centre on developing the individual's own human ability for the purpose of achieving wealth, success and happiness, with Jesus and the power of his resurrection left out.

I also knew by now of other pitfalls in commercial ventures. I had seen how easily the drive for profit could become the only focus—could even flow into human greed—and how easy it was for people to let their priorities become unbalanced. My desire was to learn to maintain God's priorities in my life: God first, family second and business third. I also hoped to inspire others to the same ideas. I wanted no part in greed.

Persuaded, though, that God's purpose for me was indeed to relaunch my career in business, I rang the executive and accepted his offer. He had wanted me to sign a three-year consulting contract. I recalled my impression on my way to the Beulah Retreat Centre of 'two years', hesitated in my decision, but finally agreed to the contract the executive proposed.

When I got settled in Dallas I telephoned my friend Patti and told her about my new life in Jesus. She was delighted to hear this news and also that we now lived in the same city, and she asked what I was doing that evening. I told her I was going to a seminar at Word of Faith Outreach Centre in Farmers Branch.

'I don't believe it!' she exclaimed. 'That's where *I* go to church!'

It turned out that both of us had been attending this church without seeing each other. We agreed to meet there that night. Following the service we had coffee together. I told her that my conversion had come on June 11, 1978.

'Now I understand what was happening to me then,' she said. 'The week before your conversion I was awakened *twice* in the middle of the night with a heavy burden to pray for you. I got out of bed and got down on my knees before God in intercession. I had no idea what you were going through; I just knew something important was happening.'

For the first time that evening it came home to me how Patti had been used by God to intercede faithfully for me—for more than nine years. What was more, I found that she was the one who, during her visit to my house in Florida, borrowed my Bible and felt inspired to take a purple pen and underline those verses in Isaiah.

Shortly afterward I hired Patti as my personal secretary in the company we were setting up to market the hydroculture plants. In the firm's first two months we developed the marketing plans, then decided to buy out a Houston-based competitor, which, curiously, had as staff many people whom I had trained in my 1975 project in Florida. This purchase gave my firm immediate distribution and a sales network in five cities in Texas and Louisiana. I questioned, however, whether the planned capitalisation would be adequate for the long term, and I was assured that it would be. Once again, the business horizon looked promising.

In the beginning of my new work in Dallas I was hesitant about telling my associates and subordinates about Jesus and what he had come to mean to me. I held back my testimony even at opportune moments. Then, as I confessed my hesitancy and insecurity to the Lord, he began to set me free to speak about the things of God. Boldness entered my heart and I did speak about Jesus, first with one person, then with another and another.

Moreover, I tried to base everything in the corporation's life on principles from scripture. When we held leadership training classes I also taught spiritual principles from God's Word.

Four of our five districts had a husband and wife team as manager, and one had a single woman as manager. As I worked with these people, I would often share my faith—not without challenges to my own new life in the Spirit.

One district manager couple, as they joined the company in spring 1979, had come to question the validity of the Charismatic Renewal. The wife brought me three books, lent by her pastor, written against the renewal; she felt the Lord had sent her into the company to lead me out of the charismatic experience. I read each of the three books carefully, because I knew what it was to have a false set of beliefs and I never wanted to be in that position again. One book in particular was well written and convincing, and it took me six months to regain total confidence that the renewal was truly the work of the Holy Spirit.

This assessment gave me new understanding and compassion for brothers and sisters from parts of the Body that had doctrinal ideas about the Charismatic Renewal different from those I had come to adopt. I could see that if I had been taught as they had been, and had read books against the renewal before I received the baptism in the Holy Spirit, I too would have had serious reservations about entering the charismatic dimension.

All the manager couples were already Christians, except one husband, who later came to a point of surrendering his life to the Lord. Subsequently all four men and five women —including the husband and wife who had tried to draw me away from the charismatic expression—received the baptism of the Holy Spirit and the gift of tongues. These faith steps had a ripple effect and many others were soon touched by God's love. We prayed for the Lord to heal people and saw him do it in our midst. We saw others converted to a love relationship with Jesus.

'Ah, Lord,' I said one day, '*now* I see! It is in the business world that I will fulfil my mission for you.' The fruits, after all, were quite clear. But, as events would later show, I was wrong.

In October 1979 I went with a friend to her church in Garland, Texas—the International Christian Centre (ICC). During my first visit to this interdenominational charismatic church, I received in the course of the service a second prophecy telling me again that God had a call on my life. The prophecy came through the church's pastor, the Rev Marvin Crow.

A month later, while I was having a quiet time with the Lord in my bedroom, it felt as if God's hand gently picked me up and moved me from Word of Faith Outreach Centre to ICC. I didn't understand why; for eighteen months I had been faithful in attending Word of Faith and had been very blessed. The transition took me from a body that had grown to 1,500 who worshipped together each Sunday to a fellowship of three hundred. As I was to find out, however, God had developed International Christian Centre into a training ground for new ministries. It was from ICC in fact that the pastor of Word of Faith had been ordained and first sent forth.

I also found myself part of a more intimate church family. I came to know many more people, and more personally, and was brought into a deeper Christian community life.

Marvin Crow, the pastor, a fiery preacher and a man with great compassion and wisdom, now became my spiritual counsellor. At that point Marvin had been a pastor in the Charismatic Renewal for twenty-five years.[15] He had begun as a Baptist pastor and, following his experience with the baptism in the Holy Spirit in the mid 1950s, was forced to leave his denomination; he then moved to the interdenominational sphere.

The company I was directing, meanwhile, was growing well but it was young and fragile. In the spring of 1979 the United States was hit by a serious petrol shortage. This had a disastrous effect upon the corporation, because our hydroculture plants were sold primarily through gatherings of women in their own homes, what we called 'the party plan'. With everyone skimping on petrol wherever they could, non-essential car trips were being cancelled. It was difficult

---

[15] In the 1950s in the United States a move of the Holy Spirit swept through various Protestant churches, though it was not until the early 1960s that this move came to be called 'the Charismatic Renewal'.

for our sales force to obtain enough fuel to get to their appointments. Consumers stopped driving to home demonstrations to save on petrol. Our sales went into a tailspin and some of our sales force quit.

My associates and I did everything we could over the next eight months to pull the company out of its downward spiral. The fuel shortage had caused a great deal of damage. Nothing that we tried worked quickly enough. I could see that my concerns about under-capitalisation had, after all, been realistic.

It became evident early in 1980 that we would have to restructure the company. One thought was to find a buyer and sell the company to obtain additional capital needed to continue. Another idea was to create a marketing system with independently controlled distribution centres, instead of company-controlled centres.

We examined both options. When a buyer could not be found, we decided on the second one, the creation of independent distribution centres. The district managers were offered the chance to take over the operations of their centres as independent business people; all of them decided to do this. This meant the phasing out of the home office, and the premature termination of my contract at about the two-year point.

The changeover began on April 1. I continued in my post for another month to help with details of the transition; at the end of April I was to depart. I was somewhat anxious about my life, not having any idea what would come next.

For a while it appeared that I would purchase an interest in one of the distribution centres. Indeed, I had even pledged commitment of personal capital. My financial commitment was tied to my interest in real estate that my father and I then had up for sale. The property had been on the market for nine months but was showing no sign of being sold very quickly, so I felt secure in using it as collateral. In the meantime I would be able to secure financing from other sources.

On April 30, much to my surprise, my participation in the project was refused.

I called out to the Lord, saying, 'God, I don't understand this!' For over a month I had tried to hold this business door open. It took a lot for the Lord to get across to me that it was he, not the enemy, who was shutting the door on this project.

On May 1 my father phoned me to tell me that the property had been sold—just one day after I was released from my commitment of the money this sale would bring. My part of the money could now be used to finance this interim period.

It was a time of living in uncertainty. I kept knocking at every possible open door, checking every direction, not knowing what the next step in my life would be. I looked into two other business opportunities but decided neither held any promise.

My pastor at ICC, the Rev Marvin Crow, had begun to ask me, during my counselling sessions with him, if it was not possible that God was calling me into full-time evangelistic service. Curiously, considering my long-held conviction of being called to serve the multitudes, my first response was 'no'.

'How,' I asked Marvin, 'could I, a single mother of two teenage boys, go from the business world into full-time ministry without any training, with little understanding of how to preach? How would I be able to take care of and provide for my sons?'

I could see no way to make such a transition.

8

Forgiving

Then the financial picture changed again—for the worse. Two men who owed my corporation a large debt, which I had counted on receiving in this period, refused to pay. Their refusal caused a catastrophe for me. I found an anger in me toward these men that was so great that I could think of nothing but what they had done to me. Within a week I could feel this anger turning to bitterness in my spirit. As I reeled from one financial crisis to another, each crisis fanned the flames of that bitterness.

So consumed were my thoughts by this anger that I found I had little time for God. Something, I knew, had to change. But what? It became obvious that nothing in my debtors' attitude was going to change. The only possible change had to come inside of me—and I was the one who had been wronged by abuse of trust. I knew I had to forgive, but I didn't know *how* to forgive, and I cried out to the Lord, 'I know you tell me to forgive, and I want to forgive, but all I feel is anger. Please help me!'

A week later while reading scripture I began to receive an answer. It came from the gospel of Matthew. During my time of reading, this verse seemed to jump off the page, and came to life in my heart:

'But I say unto you, Love your enemies, bless them that curse you, do good to them that hate you, and pray for them which despitefully use you . . .' (Matthew, 5.44, KJV).

I did not, however, know exactly what to do with this scripture.

The more I contemplated these verses the more I saw I could begin to do something: I could bless my debtors and pray for them. I couldn't understand how doing these things would help me to forgive, but I knew that God was speaking to my heart, telling me to be obedient to his Word.

I found something else. At the moment I opened my mouth, God showed me my heart. Saying 'Bless their families, Lord: bless them individually,' did not strike me as particularly difficult to say. But when I said, 'Bless their businesses, Lord, make them prosper financially,' I saw what was on my heart, and it wasn't pretty. God let me see that I did not *want* their businesses blessed; I did not *want* them to prosper financially. What I really wanted was for them to have just as many problems as they had caused me—or, better, *even more* problems.

In short, what I was saying with my lips and my intellect did not match what was in my heart. I was saying, 'I want to forgive,' but God revealed to me my heart—a heart still hardened against forgiveness.

I prayed these prayers for one week, for two weeks . . . nothing happened. All I could feel was bitterness and anger. I prayed for three weeks, four weeks. Again, nothing. I began to say, 'Lord, this doesn't work! I still feel anger and bitterness.' And the only thing I experienced from God was an inner urging that said, 'Keep going, be obedient to my Word.' In six weeks there was still no change.

The seventh week brought a breakthrough. One day as I was praying, the words I was speaking became ignited with faith, and I experienced a love for the two men who had hurt me; for myself, I experienced God's healing love through the forgiveness I had tendered out of obedience. It was very dramatic. Suddenly I was free from anger. It no longer mattered that those men had not paid me what they owed (and, indeed, they never did). Through the power of the Holy Spirit I had forgiven them.

But it was a beginning . . . and only a beginning . . . in my learning how to forgive.

The Lord, through this lesson, let me see that there is no true life of faith without obedience. And no discipleship without it, either. So many times we like to live in comfortable compromise: We want to submit ourselves to the Lord in a *conditional* discipleship. 'I'll do what you want Lord so long as . . .' or 'on condition that . . .'

What this attitude means, in the long run, is that we want to do God's work *our way, not his*. As this reality became clear in my heart, it went very deep. Finally, it struck me: If Christ is not Lord over *all* of your life, he is not Lord *at all*.

During this interim period I made a mistake in judgment —lingering over considering a business project about which I had serious ethical questions. I knew I should shut it out of consideration immediately, but I hesitated. I sought God in repentance for this error. And I received his forgiveness and was reconciled with him.

I had no question in my heart that God had forgiven me. The next day and the day after, however, I continued to feel a burden and guilt for my sin. I didn't understand why. This feeling went against my past experiences with God's forgiveness which had at other times brought freedom from guilt. On the third day, the burden, now heavier than ever, drew me into a time of seeking an understanding.

'I know I've been forgiven,' I cried to the Lord. 'Your Word tells me that if I confess my sins, you are faithful and just to forgive me and cleanse me from all unrighteousness. Why do I still *feel* so guilty?'

As I prayed in my room, an understanding began to take shape in my heart. In that small, still inner voice through which God often speaks to us there came these words: 'My daughter, I have forgiven you; but you have not received my grace fully. You have not forgiven yourself.' Then another sentence: 'Who do you think you are in not forgiving yourself when I, your Almighty God, have forgiven you?'

I learned a valuable lesson: that which the Holy Spirit had placed upon my heart was true and there was a spiritual pride working within me at that moment—not accepting God's forgiveness, manifested by my not forgiving myself. This taught me more about guilt and the feelings it produces. I also learned about the difference between 'conviction' and 'condemnation.'[16] The Holy Spirit convicts our hearts and draws us to repentance. After we repent, if we still feel guilt, it is often a sign that we have not accepted God's grace in its fullness. By not forgiving ourselves, we leave a door open for Satan to spark thoughts of self-condemnation and unworthiness. Rather, we should all heed the advice that Paul wrote to the Romans: 'There is therefore now no condemnation to them which are in Christ Jesus, who walk not after the flesh but after the Spirit. For the law of the spirit of life in Christ Jesus hath made me free from the law of sin and death' (Romans 8.1–2, KJV).

Later, when my ministry was well under way and had

---

[16] See John 16.8–11.

become international, old wounds would begin to surface, wounds I had buried deep inside of me. I would need to learn even deeper lessons about forgiveness. And God would teach me more.

9

Three books

In June 1980, still in the uncertainty of not knowing where my future lay, I went to visit the farm in North Carolina. I liked this place: I could walk by myself through fields of corn or in the woods or just sit on a swing in the big backyard and reflect on my life. Nothing in my life over the past ten years, I came to see, had been very ordinary. I had lived everything at a fast pace, obtaining what the world called 'success' but finding that position, prestige and material abundance felt tinny, and were no longer valuable.

While on the farm I read a book that dealt with how God changed people's names in biblical times. I saw, for example, that God told 'Abram' that 'neither shall thy name any more be called Abram but thy name shall be Abraham; for a father of many nations have I made thee' (Genesis 17.5, KJV). Among many others there were changes such as 'Sarai' to 'Sarah', 'Simon' to 'Peter' and 'Saul' to 'Paul'. The book also explained that God changed names for specific purposes.

I asked myself then if my changing of my name from 'Phyllis Ann' to 'Kimberly' had been more than a personal decision. What, after all, did 'Kimberly' mean? I didn't know.

Upon arrival back in Dallas by plane I went immediately to the public library and went through various books to see if I could locate the meaning of 'Kimberly'. It should have been easy because Kimberly was a very popular name in America then, but I could not find it anywhere. I did however find a book with the name 'Kim' in its listings. The origin of 'Kim' was given as Anglo-Saxon and its meaning as 'glorious leader'.

From the time I had taken the name of 'Kimberly' indeed I had always used the short form of 'Kim' and that's what everyone called me. Moreover, under this name I always held leadership positions (even if they weren't 'glorious'). This research led me to think that my name change had possibly been part of God's plan. I also had the thought, 'How glorious it is to lead people to Jesus!'

On June 11, 1980, on my way home from a midweek evening service at International Christian Centre, I felt the Holy Spirit impressing on my heart that I should obtain and read two books that I had already heard about: *Daughter of Destiny*, the story of Kathryn Kuhlmann, and a book called *A Christian Love Story*. Kathryn Kuhlmann had died in 1976. I knew only vaguely that she was considered, as her biography declared, 'the foremost woman evangelist of the century'. In her fifty years of ministry she was said to have 'witnessed to her Lord's love and power before a hundred million people'. The other book, by Zola Levitt, who referred to himself as 'a Hebrew Christian', was even more of an enigma. I would find that it told of the Jewish marriage customs current at the time Jesus walked the earth.

The next morning I went down to the store in the little town of Rockwall where I lived and, rather amazingly, was able to find both books in the small Christian book section there. I bought them and took them home.

I began by reading *Daughter of Destiny*, Kuhlmann's official biography written by Jamie Buckingham. By the end of the first chapter I had noticed similarities between the family backgrounds of Kathryn Kuhlmann and Kim Kollins. These were so striking that, a bit flustered, I began to reread the chapter. First of all I saw that her mother's name was Emma; that was also my mother's name. Her father's name was Joseph, and that was my father's middle name. I noticed that the middle names of her grandparents on her father's side were Maria and Heinrich; those were the first names of my mother's parents. Kathryn's grandparents were Lutheran; so were mine. Hers came from Westphalia in northern Germany, not far from Buxtehude, where my grandparents had lived.

As I checked off these similarities I really did not know what they could mean. But I was afraid to speculate or to go any further in the book.

Around ten o'clock that evening, while I was on the phone talking to my friend Patti and relating to her what I had discovered that day, there came a strong presence of what I perceived as God's glory in my room. It was as if the entire atmosphere of the room had changed, and I could see in the Spirit, at the left side of my bed, a small box. I felt these words on my heart, 'In that box is the anointing for a double portion[17] of a miracle ministry that I am calling you to. Receive it, prophesy it over yourself.'[18]

I stayed on the phone with Patti throughout the experience, describing to her just what was going on. When the revelation seemed to be complete, I said, 'Lord, if this is your plan, then I know there is no way in my own strength that I can bring about a ministry wherein miracles occur except through the power of your Holy Spirit. I know you say you will confirm the proclamation of your Word with "signs following".'[19] So I surrender myself to you; and I say yes.'

After saying good-bye to Patti I said to myself, 'I'm not telling anybody else about this until I see the first miracle.' Several days later, however, I did share the experience I had had with my pastor, Marvin Crow.

---

[17] See 2 Kings 2.9. [18] Meaning 'declare it, speak it out, in faith.' [19] See Mark 16.15–20.

10

An old red boat

A few days afterwards I had a strong urge to reread the
poems I had written in 1970, not having looked at them for
many years. What I found in my verse surprised me: I
realised that the Holy Spirit must have been working
through me even then, though I was not consciously aware of
his presence. One of the poems, written that July, seemed to
foretell the ten-year spiritual journey I had just completed.

> As I walked along the shore,
>   I saw an old red boat
> On its mast it had a small white sail,
>   so weatherbeaten, so old . . .
> But in that boat a journey I had to take.
>   I looked for but found no seats;
> Then I knew through this journey
>   I would need to stand,
>   stand tall and defy them all.
> I pushed the boat off from shore
>   and into it I climbed
>   and sailed off into the deep.
> Dark storms came and made it oh so rough,
>   but I told them that me they could not touch.
> Try as they would, I would not fall;
>   they tried and they tried,
>   but I defied them all.
> As the darkness rolled away
>   and the sun broke through,
> I could see the shore
>   and my spirit's dreams come true.

My first awareness that I had a mission to fulfil had been
in 1970. During this ten-year period, how the powers of
darkness had tried to coax me into accepting the illusions of
the worldly life! Satan and his demons had tried to weave a
web around me and smother me in darkness. However, the

light of Christ broke through to illuminate the path that the Lord had marked out for my life.

In the same period I read *A Christian Love Story*. It was impressed upon me that, just as in the experience of the seven-day bridal chamber, discussed in the book, God was calling me to go away with him for seven days of fasting and stillness. I consulted my pastor about the idea and, after a discerning prayer with me, he confirmed it and encouraged me to carry it out. On the church camp grounds stood two trailers. I closeted myself in one of the trailers, staying there all alone from June 28 to July 5. Each night I read the account of the Last Supper from the gospel of Matthew and partook of a communion of bread and grape juice.[20] In those seven days I committed myself to Jesus and to him alone, entering into a relationship with him as my husband.

It did not occur to me then that this commitment would have a radical impact upon my human hope of having an earthly husband with whom I could walk in holy pilgrimage. But it would—as God's unfolding guidance would one day show.

God also made me see that he was sending me forth in a walk of faith, and that the path would not be easy. 'Through faith,' he impressed upon me, 'believe that I will fulfil your every need.' I also received the grace to enter into the calling that God had prepared for me. Moreover, as my business career, which began in a local area, then became regional and finally international, God showed me that my ministry would develop in the same way.

I had thought that God must have prepared some small country church as the place for me to begin, that possibly Marvin knew some pastor who would invite me. My heart soon let me see that God had other plans. I received an understanding that I would be organising evangelistic

---

[20] Various churches do not use wine for communion but substitute grape juice. Frequently, these are churches where drinking of any alcoholic beverages by members is discouraged.

crusades, travelling from one place to another, and praying with many hurting people.

I was to go forth in the way he had first sent Kathryn Kuhlmann forth in her ministry: I was to go into a city to find a location, such as a hotel convention room where I could hold services. Although always in submission to my home church, sent out, that is, as 'an evangelist', I was to have total responsibility to organise and lead the crusades and raise the finances. As things developed, however, I was always to plan the crusades in close consultation with the charismatic churches in each area.

Before I ever ministered anywhere else, however, I was, rather improvisationally, to help minister to the congregation that had nourished me. This came about the day after I finished my seven days of stillness in the camp grounds. During the Sunday evening service at ICC, Pastor Crow introduced me to the congregation as 'a fellow minister of the gospel'. At the service's end he whispered in my ear, '*You* close the service! Be sensitive to the moving and the anointing of the Holy Spirit; draw in the nets as he leads so that no fish will escape.'

I knew what he meant. Many times, as a member of the congregation, I had experienced the breaking through of the Holy Spirit's power, glory and anointing. Often, too, I had seen how, in the midst of this time, hearts were opened to receive graces from the Lord.

Now I was on the other side, no longer sitting in the congregation but, rather, called to close the service. Could I really experience the Holy Spirit's leadings? Could I move under his anointing? It struck me that I just had to be willing to step out of my 'boat' and trust God to help me 'walk on the water'. If, indeed, God was calling me to proclaim his gospel, then his grace would be with me.

As I took the microphone into my hand my feelings of fear and apprehension melted away. I suddenly felt the tenderness of God's love. Entering into prayer I could feel in my heart the impulses for each step of what I was to do and say. I found myself issuing an invitation to all to surrender their lives anew to the Lord and open their hearts to receive his delivering and healing power. People began to rise and come forward to receive prayer, many with tears streaming down their faces. As others and myself prayed with them, it was exciting for me to see the Holy Spirit working in their hearts and lives.

11

'You've never loved me!'

In the business world I had come to enjoy financial success and security through the corporation that I had owned. Now I was to leave that way behind me and walk in a brand new way. As I told my sons I was preparing to enter full-time service for God, Robert asked, 'How is this going to work? How are you going to support us financially? How will we live?' I tried to explain that God would be our source in everything, but his questions only became blunter; 'Who is going to pay the rent? Who is going to buy our food? Where will our money come from?'

I could not be more specific with him than simply to repeat that God would provide all the resources—though I did not know how.

In July a couple from ICC gave me a cheque for 500 dollars, the first gift for the ministry. I did not know what to do with this cheque—whether, for example, I was to tithe ten per cent of it. Moments later I did feel led to tithe.[21] So I immediately contributed fifty dollars to the church. The next day I felt God was asking me to give it *all* away. I felt in my heart that as I was faithful to give back to God the first financial fruits of the ministry to which I had been called, he would be faithful to meet all my needs.

On July 16, 1980, the day of my being blessed as a minister

---

[21] Tithing is an Old Testament principle. See Leviticus 27:30–33.

of the Gospel of Jesus Christ, I asked both my sons to attend this Wednesday evening service with me; I told them it would be an extremely important event in my life. I would receive the laying on of hands of my pastor and the congregation to be sent forth in the ministry of evangelisation. Both refused to go. I felt very hurt. All day I tried to persuade my elder son to go with me that evening and we got into a big argument. We both ended up crying.

'Son,' I finally said, desperate for some resolution, 'I love you.'

Robert wheeled around and shouted at me, 'You don't love me. You've never loved me!'

Dashing into my bedroom in tears I collapsed on the bed and cried, 'Lord, this is not from you! I need your help!'

The impression I received on my heart, though, was not to my liking. 'Kim,' it felt the Lord was saying, 'you are wrong.'

'What do you mean, I'm wrong?' I pleaded. 'Don't you understand, Lord, how important this evening is to me, how much I desire that both my sons be there with me?'

He showed me, however, that it was my motivation that was wrong, that I did not want my sons to be there for what they could receive from God, but only to show them off to the congregation. Crestfallen, I realised that God was right on the mark. What I felt he wanted me to do was to go and ask Robert for forgiveness. Something I had never done before in all my years as a mother.

I left the shelter of my bedroom and sought out my son.

'Please, son, will you forgive me?' I said.

'For what?' he said, thoroughly startled at my request.

'Because I was wrong in trying to pressure you to come to church tonight. I can see now that I only wanted you there to show you off, not for what you might receive from God.'

Robert said yes, he would forgive me, and he began to weep.

Neither of my sons was to go to the service that day in which I would be sent forth as an evangelist, but I accepted that well. The important thing was that the wall between us had come down, and God's peace had returned to our home.

55

12

Tyler, Texas

After prayer, I felt that Tyler, Texas, was where the first crusade was to be held. I also sought God's guidance on how long the crusade should last; what came to me very strongly was 'three weeks, with two services a day'. This length of time went totally against the norm; if a meeting continued over three or four days, that was considered long. To go to a city without anyone knowing you, to rent a location and to promote a crusade for three weeks was considered highly unrealistic. Except I didn't know this at the time.

While I was preparing for this crusade I had to go to Tyler to scout a location. I knew it would not be easy to find a place for a three-week period. On my way down to Tyler that afternoon, Tuesday, July 22, I had to make a stop in a place twenty miles outside Tyler. As I was riding along a country road I noticed a truck parked just ahead of me; I saw a man standing behind the truck with a dog and two puppies, then I watched the man walk around the side of the truck and get in.

'Oh, no!' I thought suddenly, 'he's not going to leave that dog and those two puppies there, is he?'

But that's exactly what he did; he drove the pickup truck off, leaving the dogs on the road.

As I drove past the dog and the puppies I asked myself, 'Should I do something?' Then the thought, 'But what? How?' I was on my way to Tyler to find a place for an evangelistic crusade and, besides, I had two dogs of my own at home. The only solution was to pick up the three dogs, take them to an animal shelter and hope that they might be adopted.

Against my more rational judgment something in me made me stop. I turned my car around and drove back to try to find the animals. I saw the puppies still standing just where they had been left; their mother had gone off. I parked my car, got out and went to pick up the puppies. As I picked up the first puppy I was shocked. I dropped it as soon as I had picked it up. 'It's diseased,' I said to myself, sadly. Then I realised it was completely infested with ticks and fleas. Around its little feet and ears were more ticks than I had ever seen on any dog before.

Yet, I thought, 'What can I do? If I put the puppies in my car, the car will soon be full of ticks and fleas.' However I was quite taken by the little puppy with its pink tongue wagging in and out. It looked so needy and hopeful that I picked it up and put it on the back floorboard, then got the other puppy, which was equally infested with parasites, and put it in my car too.

Now the question was, 'Can I find the mamma dog?' I started to drive slowly. Glancing down a side street I spotted the puppies' mother. I turned down the side road, stopped the car, and got out and called for her to come. She balked. Then I showed her one of her puppies and she padded right up to the car and hopped in. She got into the back on the floorboard with her puppies, but she didn't stay there. The mother was a medium-sized brown and white dog and quite frisky. Before long she had jumped into the front seat next to me. The problem was that she too was infested with ticks and fleas. Now I had them right in front with me.

(Jesus, it struck me then, accepts us just as we are, taking us into his arms all bedraggled and dirty and sin-infested. He does not ask that we clean ourselves up first before we present ourselves to him—only that we come with a repentant heart. Then Jesus will cleanse us.)

I was stymied. What to do with this mess? I knew I had an appointment to make and obviously couldn't take the tick- and flea-ridden dogs with me; but I also knew that in the sweltering July east-Texas heat I couldn't leave the dogs in the car either. I thought, 'Maybe I can find somebody who will look after the dogs for a while and let me come back and pick them up.' It was evident that before I could deposit them at a shelter I would have to clean them up. Otherwise nobody would adopt them, and I wanted them to have the best chance possible of winning a new home.

Just then I saw an elderly man working on his front lawn. 'Maybe he'll do it,' I thought. I knew my request would be a strange one, no matter who I asked. I pulled into the man's driveway and stopped my car.

'Sir,' I said, 'could I ask you a *big* favour?' And I explained how the dog and the puppies had been abandoned and asked if I could leave the animals with him for at least an hour.

'Fine,' he said. 'No problem.'

'They're really a mess,' I apologised.

'That's OK,' he rejoined. 'Just leave them with me.'

I went and had my meeting, which took about ninety minutes. As I left the meeting a thought crossed my mind, 'Why should I go back for the dogs? Haven't I done enough already? Aren't they better off where they are now than where they were abandoned on the road?' It would be so much easier just to leave them with the man. How was I going to get them cleaned up? However, I made the decision to go back and retrieve them and even came upon a small store where I could obtain flea and tick powder.

As I arrived at the man's house I found a pleasant surprise waiting for me. While I was gone the man had dipped all three dogs in anti-tick-and-flea solution, given them baths and thoroughly cleaned them up. They really looked beautiful. The man said, 'If you don't mind, I'd be pleased to keep all three.' Under my breath I said, 'Thank you, Lord!'

But there was also another impression on my heart, a very strong one: that the man and I should pray together. I didn't know whether the man was a Christian or not. Normally I would not just ask a stranger outright if he wanted to pray with me. The impression, however, was so strong that I felt urged to say, 'Sir, I have this impression upon my heart that it would be good if we prayed together. Would you be willing to do that?'

'Well,' he answered, 'I'm a Christian, that's fine; let's pray.'

'Is there any particular need that you would like to pray about?'

'Yes, there is. Four days ago I was released from the

hospital after they had diagnosed a stomach tumour that was cancerous. They told me it was inoperable.'

The man was in his seventies. So we prayed together and I shared a bit about Jesus and about the experience of the Baptism of the Holy Spirit and the gift of tongues.

'Would you be open to receive these gifts from the Lord?' I asked.

He told me that one time while he was attending a Baptist church he had had an experience with the Lord and had begun to pray in strange sounds, but nobody could explain it to him very well. I told him that I believed that probably he had already received the experience that I had described to him.

'But let's pray,' I suggested, 'and ask the Lord to liberate the fullness of the Holy Spirit in you, his love and his power.'

We were sitting outside on a wooden swing suspended from a tree and God sent such a special anointing of his love to rest upon us. Ah, the tenderness of the Lord. After we finished praying, I shared with him the plans for the crusade in Tyler and told him I would come back to pick him up one evening if he would like to attend a service. Driving away I found myself in awe of what I had just been a part of, and how simply by following an impulse to rescue an abandoned dog and two puppies, I had been able to meet and pray with that very special man.

I abandoned my plans to drive into Tyler that day, returning instead to my home outside Dallas. Without any distractions from other activities I wanted to hold onto the wonderful experience with which the Lord had just blessed me.

The next day, I set out for Tyler again to look for a location and also to visit a local congregation and tell its pastor how I saw the crusade. He was a pastor whom my pastor, Marvin Crow, knew well. This pastor was aghast that I was scheduling a crusade for three straight weeks, but he did not say anything to me. Instead, he called Marvin and asked him why he had not counselled me better. Marvin, however, replied that he felt that the Holy Spirit was leading me and he was giving me room to follow those leadings. Marvin also helped do the layout for the promotion of the crusade and for the radio spots.

The crusade was to begin on August 9. On August 6 I went to Tyler and began to visit local groups to share my vision of the evangelistic crusade. Each night until the crusade opened I shared with a different church group.

On the first evening of this first crusade, five minutes before I was to walk to the microphone to begin, I received a telephone call from Dallas saying that my son Robert, who at the time was nineteen, was being rushed to the hospital. There were no details. I did not know if he had been in an accident or seriously injured or what. So with this news on my heart I had to greet the people and start to lead my first service, making no mention of what I had just heard about my son.

The service began with praise and worship, followed by my proclaiming the Word of God, and then prayer time for individual needs with laying-on of hands. The service went well and I managed to stay focused on what God wanted to do with me right in that room. Afterward, I found out that Robert had been taken to the hospital with a severe case of influenza and a high fever, and after receiving treatment had been sent home. After the service I was able to talk with him by phone. Thus the 'crisis' turned out to be minor.

13

In faith, trusting

What I went through during those three weeks was amazing. First of all I was astonished to find out how many services I would be holding: forty! Up to this point I had preached only once before. I had to be open to prepare and deliver messages for forty times of sharing. Each afternoon I would ask the Lord to give me a theme for that evening. After the first week, when I would ask the Lord for a theme, nothing would come. No inspiration at all. I found myself having just to stand up when the time came to minister, not having the slightest idea what was going to come out of my mouth. And so I was learning very quickly what it meant to rely totally on the Lord, trusting him to fill my mouth with his words.

Among the words impressed sharply on my heart during that first crusade were, 'It is only the beginning . . .'. That seemed logical enough; it was, indeed, the beginning of my ministry. As I was to discover over the years to follow, however, that was only a part of what the Lord meant to convey.

I began the crusade in Tyler with the music ministry only partially arranged. I myself had no special talent for music and was not even, at that point, able to carry a tune. A Christian sister came from another town to lead the time of praise and worship; however, she could stay only for the first four days. Then God provided a young man aged seventeen from Tyler who helped me as praise and worship leader for the next two and a half weeks. If God calls you to do something, I was learning, then he will provide everything you need to accomplish your mission—help through others in the form of music or finances or whatever.

On the first Tuesday my pastor, Marvin Crow, and his wife Jean, an ordained minister and his co-pastor, came to the crusade to see how their newly sent-forth evangelist was doing. That same night the man who had adopted the puppies also attended the service. It was a joy to see them, all three of them.

My services for the crusade were in the morning at 10.0 and in the evening at 7.30, and on Sundays at 3.0 in the afternoon. That gave me Sunday evening free. So at the end of the first week I attended a Sunday evening service at a nearby inter-denominational charismatic church. When the time came for individual prayer, I went forward. What was prayed for, with the laying on of hands, was that God's Holy Spirit would be stirred within me and that his anointing and power would be more dynamically manifested in the ministry he had called me to. The next thing I knew I had fallen gently to the floor. (This occasion, however, was not the first, but perhaps the fourth or fifth time that I had experienced the phenomenon of falling 'in the Spirit' while someone prayed for me.) As I lay there I perceived in my spirit the Lord saying, 'You will see my power and glory liberated in your ministry, and this phenomenon will also occur.'

Monday morning as I began to pray for people, there was a noticeable difference—a stronger radiance of God's glory. Moreover, no longer did most people remain standing when I prayed for them. They fell gently and found themselves resting on the floor. Though the experience itself was not new to me personally, what was new was that, to my astonishment, now it was occurring as I was praying for individuals. This happened even though I had made no changes in the way I prayed for people. From that day on, in my services for the next five years, what came to be called 'resting in the Spirit' would occur quite regularly.[22]

During these three weeks God increased my faith and my courage. I could see his hand on my ministry and the blessings that he was pouring forth. I knew it was not anything that I was doing in my own strength.

This crusade was marked by a dramatic breakthrough of the gifts of the Holy Spirit being manifested through me. Up

---

[22] Various terms have been used in different parts of the Body to describe this phenomenon: 'Slain in the Spirit', 'going out under the power', and others. According to Fr Francis A. Sullivan, SJ, professor of dogmatic theology at the Gregorian University of Rome: 'What happens is that some of the people, when they are prayed over, usually with the laying on of hands by the person praying, fall to the floor, and frequently remain for some period of time . . . during which they are not unconscious, but their motor and sense facilities are diminished or seem temporarily suspended.' (Francis) MacNutt prefers to call this 'resting in the Spirit'; his understanding of it is that 'it is the power of the Spirit so filling a person with a heightened inner awareness that the body's energy fades away until it cannot stand.' See *Charisms and Charismatic Renewal*, p158. And Francis MacNutt, *The Power to Heal*, Ave Maria, Notre Dame, p203.

to this point my experience in the gifts of the Spirit had been limited. I had received and practised the gift of tongues for personal prayer and praise. And over the spring, the Spirit had begun to use me in the gift of prophecy as I was praying with individuals. But I had not yet been used to give prophecies in an assembly.

Now, in this crusade, the Holy Spirit was beginning to teach me how to yield myself to be used in his gifts as he desired in a community setting. In one service I felt well up within me an inward motion, or 'unction', to speak out in tongues. I could tell that I had to make a choice: to yield to this motion or to suppress it. I chose to yield. Immediately after I spoke out the message in tongues, someone in the assembly gave an interpretation in English (through the 'gift of interpretation of tongues').[23]

Then the Lord called upon me to proclaim prophecies as I was preaching or ministering. The way I experienced this was I would feel an inward motion that the Holy Spirit wanted to use me in this gift. Often the first words would come into my thoughts. Then I would have to yield myself and be obedient to speak out that which God was placing on my heart. As I began speaking, the rest of the prophecy would come to me.[24]

I was growing in each service in understanding how better to yield to the anointing and leading of the Holy Spirit. I felt led, for instance, *not* to extend a general invitation for people to come forward for prayer. Instead I would perceive in my heart who, among those present—and there usually were from fifty to a hundred—I should invite to come up for prayer. Then I would call them out, one at a time, by some description, such as, 'that woman to the left in the blue dress', and invite them to come forward. I would not ask them what they would like me to pray for (conversion,

---

[23] See 1 Corinthians 12.10 and 1 Corinthians 14.1–33. Also consult Sullivan, *Charisms and Charismatic Renewal*, pp121–150.

[24] See same citations from 1 Corinthians as Note 23. Also consult Sullivan, *ibid*, pp91–119.

baptism in the Holy Spirit, healing, and deliverance). I simply began to pray as the Holy Spirit led my heart. (What I did not then recognise was that in this form of prayer the gifts of word of knowledge and word of wisdom were breaking through.)[25]

From the second week of the crusade it was evident that I was ministering under a very strong anointing of the Holy Spirit.

Many have asked me: What *is* an anointing for ministry? (Although, as scripture shows us, each believer has received an anointing from God for basic Christian life.)[26] As I have come to understand it, God gives an anointing to a ministry or to an office that he calls someone to stand in; the anointing is not experienced simply by someone's saying, 'I want to do this or I want to do that.' Learning how to yield yourself to the Spirit's direction is what constitutes 'ministering under an anointing'. There are several descriptions in the New Testament of how an anointing is imparted, sovereignly by God or through the laying on of hands.[27]

How can we better understand the concept of God's glory, in relation to an anointing for ministry, manifested in an assembly of people gathered for praise and worship, the sharing of the Word, and prayer?

As we look in the Old Testament, we see that in the days of Solomon when the temple had been completed, Solomon sent for the Ark of the Covenant to be brought from Mount Sion and placed in the temple. All Israel was assembled before the temple—there were so many sheep and oxen they couldn't even count them, but God's glory had still not filled his house. That glory was released through an offering of praise in unity, as told in 2 Chronicles 5. 'Then the house was filled with a cloud, even the house of the Lord; so that the priests could not stand to minister by reason of the cloud; for

---

[25] See 1 Corinthians 12.8. Also consult Sullivan, *ibid*, pp31–32.

[26] See 2 Corinthians 1.21–22 and 1 John 2.20, 27.

[27] Sovereignly: See Acts 2.1–4; Acts 4.31; Acts 10.34. Laying on of hands: See Acts 13.2–3; Acts 6.5–6; Acts 9.17.

the glory of the Lord had filled the house of God' (verse 14, KJV).

Each time I minister, my prayer is that some day a cloud of God's glory will be liberated in the same way as in 2 Chronicles 5 as we become united and offer a love gift of our praise to Jesus.

God has said that he chooses the foolish to confound the wise, the weak to confound the mighty. Yet so often when God speaks to us we say, 'Lord, I am not worthy; Lord, I am not qualified; Lord, there must be somebody else who can do this task better than I.' I said all those things to my Lord, and more, before my ministry began. When he called me out of the business world to an evangelistic ministry I said, 'My qualifications are in business, Lord. I am so young in your Word. I don't know where to start!' He showed me 1 Corinthians 1.27: 'But God hath chosen the foolish things of the world to confound the wise; and God hath chosen the weak things of the world to confound the things which are mighty.'

So I said 'Yes, Lord; I'll do what I feel you are calling me to do—and I'll trust you to guide me.' This very simple, some would say almost naïve, approach had one great advantage. Because I was not experienced in ministry, because I did not know how to preach or teach or pray with people, I had to depend wholly on the Holy Spirit to guide me in each new instance.

Inside myself I felt a greater trust building as I realised more and more that God was truly a mighty God, the same who created the universe, the same who parted the Red Sea, the same who caused Jesus to rise from the dead.

During the Tyler crusade God confirmed his Word with signs and wonders. Many people came into a personal relationship with Jesus. Many were baptised in the Holy Spirit, and various healings took place, particularly interior healings of emotional hurts, of anger, jealousy and sorrow. Many received new hope and strengthened faith to continue walking day by day with the Lord.

I also saw God's faithfulness in finances. He had instilled a spirit of generosity in the hearts of the people and thus the ministry was supplied through their 'love offerings' during the services.

Also in the midst of this crusade I underwent two serious trials on the home front. First, I had to struggle with the question of whether my son Darin should go to live with his father in Florida. Darin did not want to go, and I did not want to let him go. Darin was visiting his father while I was doing the crusade. It was a period when Darin was going through some adolescent difficulties, especially in his school work, and deep inside of me I knew he needed to be near his father. Indeed, Darin's father had offered several times to take Darin to live with him. As a mother, however, I did not want my youngest son to leave me. But, as I realised later, I was reacting purely out of my natural maternal feelings; I was not paying attention to the leadings that the Lord was placing on my heart.

For the time being I decided to keep Darin with me, arranging with a neighbouring family to look after him during my absences from home. Second, I was told that the house I was renting was being put up for sale. My two-year lease was about to expire and was not to be renewed, as I had counted on; instead I had to accept living there on a month-to-month lease, not knowing when someone might buy my dwelling and force me to move. Already a question that would later become important to me started to make itself felt: *Where was home?*

There was indeed considerable business and movement in my life. In my first three months in evangelistic service God sent me to three cities to hold a three-week crusade in each. There were 120 services conducted for his glory.

During my second crusade, in Texarkana, Texas, I began to take my eyes off the Lord and his providence and began to look at the circumstances around me and ask myself, 'How will this problem be handled?' 'Where will I get the money for this need?'

I had become so bogged down in financial and family cares, so overwhelmed by worry and overcome by fears, that

I was becoming physically and mentally drained. I would read in God's Word that I was to cast all my worries upon the Lord because he cared for me,[28] but my attempts to do that did not seem to be working. Another scripture that I meditated upon was Philippians 4.19: 'But my God will meet all your needs according to his glorious riches in Christ Jesus.' However, this scripture was not, at that moment, a reality in my life.

I soon reached a point of telling the Lord, 'God, this is just too much; you're demanding too much of me; I'm not able to walk this road of faith you've put me on. Lord, I've tried but I just cannot do it any longer.' I wanted to quit the ministry —just walk away from it and find something else to do with my life.

Each morning I would find myself waking up crying. On the fourth morning of tears I began really to cry out from the depths of my heart. 'Lord, help me! Minister to me through the time of service this morning!' And in that morning's service God was faithful and he answered that prayer. Over and over I felt these words impressed upon my heart: 'Daughter, I have sent you here to serve. First, to serve me, then to serve all those that I draw unto you. Don't look at tomorrow, nor at the day after that; look instead unto me today and to how you might be an instrument for the building of my kingdom.'

What God was telling me was a spiritual truth from Matthew 6 that I had known but that had slipped to the back of my mind: 'Therefore I tell you, do not worry about your life, what you will eat or drink; or about your body, what you will wear. Is not life more important than food, and the body more important than clothes? Look at the birds of the air; they do not sow or reap or store away in barns, and yet your heavenly Father feeds them. Are you not much more valuable than they? Who of you by worrying can add a single hour to his life? . . . But seek first his kingdom and his righteousness, and all these things will be given to you as

---

[28] See 1 Peter 5.7 and Philippians 4.19.

well. Therefore do not worry about tomorrow, for tomorrow will worry about itself. Each day has enough trouble of its own' (Matthew 6.25–27, 33–34).

That day faith was rekindled in my heart, but it was only the beginning of God's teaching me what it meant to 'let go and let God . . .'. I began to walk concentrating on just one day at a time. If I looked to next week, or next month, all the worries and fears would come tumbling back into my consciousness. If I kept focused on serving him and serving the people he had brought into the services for that day, my heart had peace.

What helped my faith considerably in this period of trial was to read over and over the complete text on God's providence in Matthew 6. And this, in effect, brought to life another biblical principle: 'Faith comes from hearing the message and the message is heard through the Word of Christ' (Romans 10.17).

Nonetheless, as I continued to move from one troubling set of circumstances to another, I would constantly find myself getting in God's way. I would frequently try to understand how God was going to work out financial problems for the ministry and our family, instead of just letting him do it. But after all *my* imagined solutions were gone, God was still God. In his sovereignty he would finally move and resolve the problem in some way that had never occurred to my imagination.

In one service an area pastor stood up and asked if he could give me a prophetic word he believed he had from the Lord. I said, 'Please do.' The prophecy he gave contained virtually the same words I had felt impressed on my heart by the Lord on the night of June 12 when I received the understanding of my calling—and I received that prophecy as a confirmation of my calling. I also felt encouraged again by the Lord's assuring me of his presence and his faithfulness.

Several days later, on Sunday September 14, a surprise awaited me. As my service was beginning, I looked up and saw my son Darin coming through the door. He had never come to see me minister before. A couple from Houston, who were friends of mine, had stopped at our house and invited Darin to come with them to my service—as a birthday present to me. I would be thirty-seven years old two days later.

On September 20 the offering contained a cheque for 1,800 dollars, enough money to pay the rental on the facilities being used for the Texarkana crusade. Worry had been useless, even counter-productive. Jesus, my Lord, was faithful.

In those first few months I learned some valuable lessons. I did not reach the point where I could walk in victory every day; it became painfully obvious that I had a lot of practising to do to keep my eyes on Jesus. Nonetheless, I had caught sight of the ideal and committed myself to working towards it. Becoming spiritually strong is not unlike becoming strong physically. It requires exercise. Unless we are ready to give ourselves to the practice of such spiritual exercise, the Word of God will not come to life in us.

As the Texarkana crusade closed, there began a week in preparation for the third crusade, to be held in October in Shreveport, Louisiana. For the third time in a row I had a scheduled three-week crusade to lead with just one week free after the previous crusade. During that one week I had to prepare for the coming crusade, including finding a large room to rent, placing the advertising in newspapers and on radio, and meeting local pastors. It took great energy and faith. Looking back I refer to this period as God's boot camp training for me. (The initial training in US military service is called boot camp.) My Lord surely wanted to toughen me for the battles ahead.

At one point I had only several hundred dollars and I felt that God was asking me to give away 180 dollars. I was obedient; I gave the money to another ministry. Then a young woman walked up to me and said, 'I feel the Lord wishes you to have this,' and she handed me a cheque for four thousand dollars. The money owed by the ministry at that time was almost ten thousand dollars, and my heart leapt over this generous gift. But the next day I felt the Lord impressing upon my heart that I was to give a thousand dollars to a family in great need. I found it much harder to give that amount away, and have three thousand dollars left, than it had been to give the 180 dollars away, and have only seventy dollars left. Often, the more money you have, the harder it is to let go of it.

In the month of November I returned to places where I had ministered earlier and held follow-up meetings for three days in each place. I had an idea that such meetings were needed for me to reinforce the themes I had preached, to comfort the people and encourage them to keep growing in their Christian life, and to keep in touch with the pastors who had supported me.

When Christmas came that first year, I again found myself in challenging financial straits. I began to sell jewellery and other valuables that I had acquired during my years as a businesswoman. Over the following years I kept up this practice of selling personal possessions to help pay for the ministry and the needs of my family. At first it really hurt me to sell my jewellery, but gradually it became easier. I thus learned how personal possessions can imprison us and hinder us in our love relationship with God. Our treasures, after all, repose in heaven, not on earth. 'For where your treasure is, there your heart will be also' (Matthew 6.19–21).

14

His alone

A non-material human treasure that I yet hoped to possess, however, was a joyous and deeply Christian marriage. After becoming a Christian I began to realise what God's plan for marriage involved, and by how much I had missed entering into that plan in my life. There was a desire in my heart that someday I might know what it was to enter and live out a marriage according to God's designs.

My first year as a Christian was spent learning how to depend totally upon the Lord to help me with the situations of daily life. And I began to realise that that probably was best for me then—not to consider marriage, so that I would not depend on someone else too soon but rather would have to depend directly, and exclusively, on God.

When, as my second year as a believer ended, I received a call to the ministry, I realised that that point was also not the time to think about marriage. Then, in the fifth month of my ministry, I underwent a period of prayer to discern what God's desire was for my life. A prophetic word spoke that God had called me to himself, and that I was to be his alone. The word reminded me sharply of the consecration I had made of myself to the Lord during my Jewish bridal chamber experience in the camp grounds that July, and drew new meaning from my vow.

Upon hearing this word, however, I felt surging up within me a tremendous amount of rebellion, and emotions unlike any I had ever felt before. It was the first time I had ever experienced a wilful rebellion against God. I was angry because I thought it was only fair that God should have revealed to me this exclusion of an earthly marriage before the ministry began, that I should have had a freedom of saying yes or no. I further felt that if it was his will for me to be single for the rest of my life, that before I accepted the call to minister I should have had clear knowledge of this vocation to a celibate life.

My rebellion lasted almost five more months. What I did not realise was that I had turned my desire to marry into an idol.

The night before Easter in 1981, just before a service, I finally said to the Lord, 'God, whatever your plan is for me, I am willing to say yes; and I will fulfil the ministry that you have called me to.' Being drawn then to this 'yes' of my heart, I also received a special grace from God to be his—and his alone. In a Protestant context this was not an easy commitment to make, because almost all the ministers and people with whom I had been in contact in ministry were married. But, unknown to me, God was already preparing my path into a church where I would meet and be comforted by many others whom he had called to walk in a celibacy consecrated to his glory.

15

Houston

For my fourth crusade, early in 1981, I had an impulse to go to Houston, Texas, to find a meeting room. This time I had a team of two others working with me in the ministry—one to help with organisation, the other to lead music—but I still did not feel ready to take on Houston. It was one of the largest cities in the United States with a metropolitan-area population of several million.

'I don't see why God has sent me to this big city,' I told a Christian woman whom I had met while making arrangements. 'I feel like a needle in a haystack.'

By way of reply she reminded me that when the Israelites arrived at the Jordan River, preparing to enter the Promised Land, God did not set them against a small city, but rather against Jericho, a great city. When I reviewed the scriptures she indicated, I definitely received the understanding that it is by the power of God, and by his power alone, that insurmountable walls come tumbling down. Houston has a large highway circling the whole city, and for me this highway became like the wall around Jericho. God's power, not mine, would topple that wall.

After looking around I found a location providing space for two and a half weeks, and scheduled the crusade. The place for the crusade lay right in the heart of a district populated by working-class blacks and Mexicans. Nearby there was also an area that was frequented by homosexuals.

The night before I was to leave for Houston, the clutch on my son Robert's car broke down. There was no money for car repairs. And this left my sons with no transportation—a fact, curiously, that was to have positive repercussions in the days ahead.

Despite these problems, I drove to Houston the next day to start the crusade. I kept telling myself, 'Keep your eyes on the Lord; don't get distracted by the circumstances.'

Though I had still not been in ministry for very long, I was by now accustomed to having thirty to fifty people appear for the first night's service. In this case, however, on the opening evening, a Thursday, no one showed up. Not a single soul.

My team and I held a prayer service anyway in which we just praised God for who he was and felt his glory liberated in our midst.

Acting on the impulse we received in response to our prayer, we decided to drive around the loop that circles downtown Houston. As we drove we interceded in the Spirit against the strongholds of darkness upon that city. And I said, 'Lord, please give us a sign. If you send just one sheep into the meeting tomorrow, just one, then I will know that this is where you want me to be.'

On Friday afternoon I received a phone call from Darin saying he had just come back from having the doctor treat him for second-degree burns inflicted on his thigh from spilling boiling water on himself. There was my excuse to cancel the crusade, if I wanted. And for most people it would have been a rather good excuse, too. But the question was: Had God called me here to do this crusade or not?

'Have I misunderstood you, God?' I prayed in my bewilderment and doubt. 'Is this the wrong place? Have I made the wrong decisions?'

That night one person came in to take part in the second evening of the crusade. I had asked the Lord to send just one as a sign, and he sent just one. Late that night, before going to bed, I prayed that the Lord would give me a contact with someone from the black and Mexican communities.

The next morning, Saturday, a black pastor who had been in the hotel on other business and noticed that an evangelistic service was scheduled came to see me. He was pastor of a church called Christian Rescue Mission, and truly God had sent him in to rescue the crusade. The minister invited me to come to his church the next day. There I shared with his people, and many responded by coming to the crusade that afternoon. That was the real beginning of a crusade that started without anyone coming at all the first night and ended up running for 88 services spanning five and a half weeks. About 4,500 people came in all.

Turbulence on the home front, however, kept up throughout the Houston crusade. Money was obtained to fix the clutch on Robert's car but within a week, Darin mishandled the car's gearbox and damaged the engine beyond repair. To replace the engine would cost over a thousand dollars, and to earn that money Robert had to move away from home and accept an offer from friends in the landscaping business. He went to live with these friends in Houston and rode with them to work each day. At the same time it became clear that I had misunderstood God the previous August as to whether I should keep Darin with me. Early in February, I sent Darin to Florida to live with his father.

Coming home tired at the crusade's close, I entered an empty house. When I left to start the crusade my household was lively; now everything had changed—both boys had gone to live elsewhere and even the two dogs had moved away (Robert had taken them with him). It really felt strange.

The next day, to compound the impression that my life was a whirlwind of change, the estate agent phoned and said it looked like the house I was leasing had been sold and I would have to vacate it in sixty days. (I waited rather uncertainly for several weeks before the agency told me that the sale had not gone through, and I would be allowed to stay.)

Though periodically my faith would waver during that first year, God was patient with me, and continued to mould me into his disciple.

16

Saving graces

My faith held quite steadfast, though, believing that both my sons would accept Jesus as their Lord and Saviour—which Darin did three weeks after the missionary woman and I claimed by faith God's promise in Acts 16.31 about my family's salvation. Now, almost three years had passed, and there was nothing to indicate that Robert was any nearer to accepting Jesus than before. To the contrary, his life seemed to have gone further away from God. He could not tolerate hearing me talk to him about Jesus. So I stopped talking about Jesus to him but continued to try to show Jesus' love in my actions towards him.

As I moved into my next crusade, this time in Dallas, Robert finished his landscaping work and moved back home, bringing with him the money to repair his car. He put the car into a repair shop, but it would be some time before the car would be ready.

He had not been back long before he and I encountered a day where there was no more food in the house, and no money to buy any. Once again I tried to explain to him that 'Our God shall supply.' He was not, however, having any more of such assurances.

'No, Mom, not *our* God!' he said and bolted from the house, slamming the door behind him. I did not know where he was going or how long he would be away. However, while Robert was off fuming, a woman who was constantly interceding phoned me to say that during her morning prayers she had had an intuition of our plight. 'I'm embarrassed to ask you this,' she said, 'but are you by any chance in need of food?' My spirit leapt over this astounding response from my Lord.

This woman invited me to come to her house immediately. When I got there I found she had waiting for me three large bags of groceries and a big box of meat. (What is more, this woman continued to supply food for my family for the next three months.) When I came home, I noticed that Robert had returned. I took one bag of groceries from the car and as I walked in the door with the bag I said, 'Son, *there's* our God!' I added: 'There are two more bags of groceries and a large box of meat in the car; will you please go and get them?'

On another occasion we had arrived at the very last day of a month and our rent payment was due. We did not have the money. That evening I ministered at a service and at the evening's end a young couple came up to me, handed me a cheque and said, 'We just sold our used truck and we want to give that money to the work of the Lord.' The cheque was written out for the exact figure of our monthly rent.

Even after the rather dramatic reprovisioning of our bare cupboards and the securing of our shelter, however, Robert kept telling me, 'It's *your* God, not mine.'

How many times did I live and see God's faithfulness to supply during my early ministry, yet how many times did I nonetheless watch faith turn into doubt? It seemed a constant uphill struggle to believe in God for everything I needed. As I grew in faith and allowed faith to be exercised in my daily living, however, the ministry became more and more stable.

During the third week of the Dallas crusade, as I was leaving for services one evening, Robert, still with no transport, wanted to go and see a friend. In his frustration, he asked me if he could drive me in my car to the service, take the car to his friend's house, then come back and pick me up later. I said 'yes, why not?' At this point Robert was still a confirmed atheist; he wanted nothing to do with God—or with my ministry.

When we arrived at the hotel where my crusade was being held, Robert came in to phone his friend. After phoning he returned to me in a disappointed mood; his friend was not home. 'What am I supposed to do now?' he said, a bit out of sorts. '. . . well,' he continued before I could make any reply, 'It's not going to hurt me if I stay and watch what you do.'

He took the last seat in the rear of the assembly, off in the remote left corner. Throughout the service I had to make sure I didn't keep throwing glances his way; I tried my best to keep myself focused on Jesus.

Then came a time in the service when I asked people to share signs of peace and love with each other, shaking hands to greet each other in the Lord. I did notice a number of people going to greet my son.

That was the first time Robert had ever experienced a service that his mother had led. He was soon to experience some others. For the next two out of three evenings we went through replays of the first night: Robert asking to drop me off and take the car to his friend's house and, twice again, his friend not being at home and Robert deciding to stay and sit through the service.

After we got home late on a Thursday evening, tired from preaching and ministering, I quickly fell asleep. About 2.0 am there came a knock on my bedroom door. Then my son's voice saying, 'Mom, can I come in?' I found it difficult to wake up. Finally opening my eyes I looked at my clock and said out loud, 'Why it's two o'clock in the morning!' Then another knock and Robert's voice again, asking if he could come in.

'OK. Come on in,' I said drowsily.

He entered the room and said simply, 'I'm ready.'

'Ready?' I thought. What is he talking about?

'You're ready for what?' I said aloud.

'To receive the baptism of the Holy Spirit.'

'First,' I replied, shaking sleep from my eyes, 'how about receiving Jesus?'

We sat down at the end of my bed and my first thoughts were, 'Lord, let me *feel* something; let me feel your presence; let me feel your anointing.' I had waited three years for this day. But I felt nothing. Then I started speaking in my heart, 'Lord, let *him* feel something. It's such an important time!'

Robert prayed a prayer of repentance in which he told the Lord that he was a sinner and asked him to forgive him for his sins, then he invited Jesus to come into his heart, and he confessed that he believed in Jesus' death and resurrection.

Following this we prayed that Robert be baptised in the Holy Spirit.

I will never forget my son's comments after this series of prayers.

'Mom,' he said, 'I didn't feel a thing. Are you sure this works?'

Reaching out to God out of my own helplessness I begged, 'Lord, help me; give me the words!' And these words came into my heart, 'Son, it is not by feelings that Jesus became your Lord and Saviour tonight. It is by faith that you have received.'

The next day we did not even talk about what had happened during the night.

On Sunday morning, however, I had a heartening experience. Coming down the stairs dressed for church, I found my son also dressed and waiting for me. 'Mom,' he said, 'this is going to sound funny, but do you mind if I go to church with you today?' That was the first time that my son Robert had willingly gone to church with me. He was baptised with water on Mother's Day of that year, 1981. What a beautiful Mother's Day present!

Sometimes when we pray, no 'spiritual feelings' appear to confirm to us that our prayer is reaching God—or that God is in the process of responding to our prayer. Our natural response is, 'I'm not communicating with God; I'm not going to receive anything from God.' But faith has no feelings. Whether we experience some feeling has nothing to do with whether we are in touch with God or receiving something from God. God *does hear us and is responding to us*, whether we can feel it or not.

After nine months of scheduling crusades in various cities, I found that God was doing something new with the ministry. I began to receive invitations to minister in churches of different denominations (but all of them open to the Charismatic Renewal) in Texas, North and South Carolina and Florida. Thus I was introduced to brothers and sisters of the

Pentecostal, Methodist, and Baptist faiths. I started to learn more about different doctrinal positions in the various churches. I soon found out that they had a variety of understandings of how to interpret and apply scripture.

I would often hear people in the Charismatic Renewal use a phrase, 'I have a check in my spirit.' Usually they meant by this that they felt that something was wrong and therefore not from the Holy Spirit. This term, with the same meaning, was often used in Pentecostal circles. I began to employ this term myself when I felt something wasn't right. I came to realise however that such a 'check' did not necessarily mean that something was not of God, only that it did not agree with my current beliefs. I learned not to judge things only by my feelings, and also that I needed to be open to submit my understandings *anew* to God's Word and the Holy Spirit, and trust the Spirit to bring enlightenment to my mind.

Though I was basically away from the crusade-style ministry in which I had begun, I did take part in this period in one evangelistic crusade held in a rented convention room in Greensboro, North Carolina—but only as an invited participant; the crusade had been organised by my friends, Ken and Rosali Edwards, of the Beulah Retreat Centre. God used the occasion, however, to put me into contact with Patrick Grace, a Beulah board member, who would soon be off to spend a year in France. I felt led to mention to him that I believed my minstry would one day become international. 'I'll be your front man in Europe,' he said jokingly. The Lord, it would turn out, was more serious about the offer than Patrick was.

Meanwhile, I could not understand why I was being invited into different churches and into other people's ministries, instead of continuing my ministry as before. What was the Lord trying to teach me? But I received no answer to my question.

One thing was clear: no longer was I in charge of the entire service. I had to be in submission to the leadership of each church where I ministered, and I had to learn to live out each service in obedience to, and unity with, their leadership.

Wherever I went into different parts of the Body of Christ, I found I could experience the love of Jesus in each part, and in each individual member. God wanted them *all* to dwell in his house.

The services were a time of praising God and sharing his Word. I used the themes of faith, a call to conversion and discipleship, renewing one's thoughts to develop the mind of Christ, a call to walk in the power of the Holy Spirit. We had always had a time for individual prayer at the end of each service.

Now, I no longer prayed for individuals by myself. The pastor of each church would stand and pray with me. I continued to call certain people to come forward for prayer, as I had during my crusades. And I would pray for them, as usual, without asking them their needs. After the services the pastors often asked me, 'Did you realise that you were praying for the exact need or problem that each person had?' I started to understand how the gifts of word of knowledge and word of wisdom were manifested in this form of prayer.

Jesus changed many lives through those services. In one instance a young man and I agreed in prayer[29] for the deliverance of his sister. She had plunged into drugs, alcohol abuse, lesbianism, and occult practices, and had come to the brink of killing herself. Through that agreement in prayer the young man's sister was, a short time later, brought to a saving knowledge of Jesus, delivered from demonic affliction and baptised in the Holy Spirit.

Some time later I received a letter from her. She was now married and expecting her first child. She wrote: 'I can honestly say that throughout this past year spent with God I have experienced a life brand new and quite different from the old . . . It is just amazing, but of course, I realise that there is absolutely no way that it would have been possible without the gracious compassion of God and the love of his precious Son Jesus Christ. And Oh! The wonderful feeling

---

[29] See Matthew 18.19.

you get when you allow God to pour his Holy Spirit into your whole intellectual being.'

Another case was that of a young man aged twenty who just appeared one evening, not knowing why; he had been on his own since he was thirteen. He too had been drawn into homosexual experiences and had had other dark involvements with drugs and occult practices. Jesus touched him that night, set him free and released in him the power of the Holy Spirit.

Then the pastor of a small South Carolina church where I was ministering asked me to visit a member of his congregation in hospital, a young woman in her twenties who had already undergone surgery three times and who was expected to die. This pastor and I prayed that the Lord would 'go before us to prepare the way'. When we arrived at her bedside the next day she told us that at 4.0 am she had awakened and prayed and cried out to the Lord for help, and God had responded by baptising her in the Holy Spirit. Then she started to glorify God in a new tongue. We laid hands on her and prayed that God's strength and healing power would flow into her. Her husband became so excited over his wife's experience that he too asked for the baptism in the Spirit.

Still another account concerns an eighteen-year-old boy who lived in a rough South Carolina village of textile mill workers. A young Christian woman spotted him sitting on the kerb near the church looking very downcast. She invited him to come to the service that night which I was to lead. We had an altar call[30] and the Holy Spirit prompted me to ask this young man to come forward that I might pray with him. At the altar that evening he committed his life to Jesus and received the baptism in the Holy Spirit. He then actually leaped into the air for joy. He confessed before the whole congregation that he had been planning to take his life that night.

After ministering at an Assemblies of God church in

---

[30] An invitation given, usually at the end of a service, for people to come forward to the altar, usually to make a public profession of faith. This practice is predominant in Baptist, Pentecostal and certain inter-denominational churches.

Hawkins, Texas, I drove back to Tyler. I was stopped in my car waiting for a red light to change to green when suddenly my car was struck from behind by a vehicle travelling at high speed. The impact propelled my car into a collision with the car in front of me. The out-of-control vehicle was a car driven by a college student who was fleeing from the scene of a previous accident, a collision of his car with a motor caravan, in which he had been at fault. When I felt the impact, I got out of my car, not thinking about whether I'd been injured, and went to the car that had hit mine. I wanted to see if the driver was all right. Passers-by were lifting him slowly out of the car and placing him on the ground. He appeared to have serious injuries and was bleeding from the head. I sat down and put his head on my lap, then began praying for the Lord to touch him. When the ambulance attendants took him away, my white dress was soaked with his blood. It was then that I realised that the left side of my face had gone numb. I was told that my car was completely undriveable and unrepairable and would have to be towed away. Shortly after the accident I went to the hospital where doctors found I had sustained injuries to my spinal column. The accident left me with pinched nerves in my arm and neck that inflicted recurrent pain upon me for the next year and a half.

It was a strange feeling to be stranded in a town ninety miles from home—injured, my car destroyed and having no way to replace it. And not knowing what I would be able to do next. The accident had occurred on the second night of a week-long revival meeting. However, the day after the accident I found someone to come and pick me up and drive me to the church. I was determined that, injured or not, I would complete the meeting.

That week-end a member of the congregation donated to the ministry a car that was ten years old, a car that would serve me well for the next seven months. Once again God had shown his faithfulness.

The accident in Tyler was only the first of three brushes with death on the road during the course of my next eighteen months of travel for God.

III
WHERE IS HOME?

WHERE IS HOME?

During the week I spent in fasting and stillness with the Lord before my ministry began in June 1980, I had an impression that the pattern of my business career would be repeated in my work as an evangelist. In business I had had seven months working on a regional level, then seven months on a national level, and in the third seven-month period I had begun to work on an international level.

One day in October 1981 in the second month of my third seven-month period of ministry, I arrived home from holding evangelistic services out of town and found a telegram waiting for me. (At this point I had no telephone because my money was so short.) Since, at times, some creditors would send telegrams to try to hasten payment on money owed, I did not open this particular telegram for several days. In fact I almost threw it away without opening it.

Finally I said to myself, 'OK. Let's just see what this is.' After tearing open the envelope I found the following message:

U INVITED MINISTER FRENCH CATHOLIC CHARISMATICS DEC. 12 13 CABLE—REPLY URGENT WITH PHONE NUMBER TIME WE CAN REACH U. PATRICK GRACE 140 AV J MERMOZ 64000 PAU FRANCE.

I told my pastor about the invitation and he said that if I felt that this was God's call, I should accept. In my prayer time with the Lord I perceived just one word: 'Go!' I did not have the money for the ticket. But that, I had learned by now, was God's problem, not mine; if he wanted me to minister in France, he would provide the resources.

I answered the telegram by confirming that I would come, before having any idea of how I was going to be able to afford to get there. Two days before I was to leave for France, having made reservations but not yet paid for my Dallas–Paris round-trip ticket, I went to the insurance company of the young man whose car had hit mine. Going alone with no legal counsel, I prayed that God would give me favour. I discussed with the company my accident claim and was astonished that they offered to settle immediately. Normally such negotiations are done by lawyers and it can take years before any settlement money is paid. I was also surprised at how much money the insurance company was proposing to pay me. They typed out a cheque that provided more than enough money for my airline ticket.

Amazingly, after just sixteen months of evangelism in my own country, I was to board a large jet and fly five thousand miles from Dallas to a small city in the foothills of the Pyrenees mountains in south-west France to proclaim Jesus' healing love.

What had happened, I learned, was that Patrick Grace and his wife Jennifer, upon arriving in Pau, had joined the local Catholic charismatic prayer group. That group was to be host for a large regional meeting drawing together prayer communities from throughout south-west France. The main speaker had had to cancel his engagement. The Pau leaders were in a quandary as to whom to invite in his place. Patrick began to talk about the kind of ministry I was conducting.

'Why don't we invite *her*?' one leader suggested. The leaders' group prayed about the idea and the other leaders felt an accord in their hearts. The Holy Spirit's impulses know no limits of distance or culture; his sovereignty is awesome.

God also carried his plan of introducing me to the different parts of the Body of Christ a giant step further: I had never before even worshipped with, much less ministered to, Catholics. And here I was, dropped into the middle of the *French* Catholic Charismatic Renewal! My ability to understand French was nil.

Jean-François Gaudeul, the priest-chaplain of the Pau group, met my flight from Paris at Pau airport, along with the Graces. I greeted him with a hug in the fashion of some American Christians and that for him was quite a surprise. In France, I quickly learned, people in the Renewal greet one another with a kiss on each cheek. Thus my first meeting with a Catholic priest included a whimsical twist.

The next day I rested at the apartment of a prayer group member, Janine du Chatelet, who spoke a little English and made me feel quite at home. The day after, a Friday, I was taken to Lourdes for lunch at the Convent of the Assumption and my first meeting with nuns. Then I was shown the grotto where the Virgin Mary was said to have appeared to a young girl named Bernadette Soubirous in 1858.

As a Protestant I had scant understanding of Mary and her role in the Catholic faith. If anything I shared an attitude common to many Protestants—scepticism.

Almost nothing that I lived through that week related to anything I had known in my ministry thus far. The language, the songs, the ways in which people expressed themselves, the order of worship (which included the first Mass I had ever attended) . . . all were strange, though beautiful.

God has wisdom, though, praise him! He blocked my intellect by putting me in a foreign context. The only way I could understand what was happening around me was with my heart. And I soon found myself falling in love with the French Catholics who had brought a Protestant woman evangelist thousands of miles from her home base to preach at their weekend assembly.

One important aspect of ministry was strikingly familiar: there was a strong presence in our midst of Jesus manifested by the Holy Spirit. Songs of praise in French filled the vaulted chapel of the Collège Saint Dominique in Pau, and hundreds of hands rose in adoration. As I stepped to a podium to begin my service, with Jill Maucorps of Bayonne as my translator, I could feel the Spirit's anointing descend on us like a dew from heaven. It was to be the first of many, many times that I would minister through translation.

Only later did I learn that along with considerable expectancy among the French charismatics over experiencing the ministry of an American Protestant woman, there had also been some reserve. Could this woman, some had been asking themselves, measure up to French standards for intellectual depth in spiritual teachings? Might she not be shallow by comparison? Then, in retrospect, I understood what the Spirit had been doing with me on the eve of my first service in Pau.

On that evening there were two teachings I was considering giving on the healing ministry of Jesus. One was quite simple and direct—the kind of teaching that would have been accepted well in many American circles. The other was long and detailed. It felt that the Holy Spirit was showing me that the second one, the long detailed teaching, would be best. I got hardly any sleep that night, so hard did I have to work to outline what I would say at St Dominique.

Following my teaching (which I found out later had been well received), the Pau leaders and I moved into a time of ministering to individual needs, the inviting of participants to come to the front for laying on of hands and prayer for whatever needs were on their hearts. Since this too involved translation from French to English, and vice-versa, we spent hours and hours in such ministry.

The music team continued to lead the assembly in songs of praise and adoration as we ministered, and, just as had occurred at most of my meetings in the United States, people began to fall gently to the floor (resting in the Spirit) as I prayed for them. For me this seemed quite usual and in order; for the people to whom I was ministering, however, this experience was completely new. Nobody seemed to have any understanding of it.

I remained in France for ten days on that first trip, visiting a Protestant community near Chalon-sur-Saone and another Catholic community, located in Paris. It was a short time for so long a journey, but one impression grew very strong inside me: that I would be back.

17

'It is well'

I flew home to Dallas and, with my son Robert, drove immediately to Florida to spend Christmas with my son Darin and my father, then 81 years old. The four of us had two wonderful weeks of family time. Then Robert and I left Florida for North and South Carolina, where I held evangelistic services in several churches. Since his conversion to the Lord, Robert had continually accompanied me on my ministerial travels. It was exciting for me to watch him grow in the Spirit. God seemed to be blessing me with opportunities to help Robert in his spiritual growth, in effect restoring to me occasions I had failed to take advantage of when my son was smaller.

Back in Texas, in mid-February, I had a weekend of ministry in a Houston church before I was scheduled to depart for Trinidad to join with a team from the Beulah Retreat Centre. This would be the first time that Robert would *not* go with me. It felt as if God was asking me to let go of Robert and trust him to take care of my elder son in my absence.

The day before I left Houston for Trinidad, however, I received an anguished telephone call from Robert. He had been going through a rough time, partly due to the break-up of his engagement with a Christian girl he had met at the time of his conversion, and he was finding it very hard to cope with life. 'Mom,' he said, 'I can't take it any more! I love you . . . and I'm sorry.' Then he hung up. And there I was, five hours from home and less than twenty-four hours from boarding a plane that would take me even further away from my son.

Can you imagine what a mother feels in such a situation?

I went straight into intercessory prayer with the pastor of the church where I was ministering and his wife, all of us on our knees. The pastor's wife felt an impression in her heart recollecting 2 Kings 4.18–36, a text that tells of the Shunammite woman who goes to Elijah because her son has died. As Elijah sees her approaching he sends his servant to ask the woman, 'Is it well with thee? Is it well with thy husband? Is it well with the child?' The woman does not respond by recounting the literal circumstances but rather by saying, 'It is well.'

The moment the pastor's wife spoke these words I felt the substance of faith come alive in my heart. The words she had voiced applied to my son. I left the next day for Trinidad, sure that God was looking after Robert and that it would be well with him.

While I was gone there was no way for Robert to reach me by phone in the area in Trinidad where the Beulah team and I were in the midst of a week's ministry in a local church. My heart kept its peace nonetheless. In the months to follow things did not get better with my son; they only got worse. Every time my thoughts turned toward Robert, the Lord reminded me of the Shunammite woman and her words of faith, 'It is well.' God's peace never left me, and Robert weathered all the storms and emerged into a much calmer, and stabler, period of his life. Indeed he would enter Midwest Bible Institute in the autumn.

An important but difficult lesson for parents to learn is to place their children in the Lord's hands and leave them there. So often I pray with parents for their children, and from my own experiences I have great faith in God's faithfulness in working in our children's lives. No problem is too big for the Lord: children's loss of faith or lack of faith in Jesus, wrong sexual relationships, drugs, depression, running away from home, suicidal tendencies. God can deal with all of these. However, one of the greatest problems is that parents let the circumstances of their children's lives dominate their thoughts and emotions. Instead of keeping their hearts focused on the promises of the Lord for their children,[31] they seem only to see the problems. They let themselves be torn apart by their worries and fears. They do not appear to realise that fear is one of the greatest enemies of faith. When fear takes root in our hearts, it chokes off our capacity to reach out to the Lord in faith.

Back in the United States after my ministry in Trinidad, I felt I was treading water. I did have some meetings scheduled in Florida churches of various denominations during March and April. But God had already anchored my heart in Europe. Father Jean-François Gaudeul and other Pau prayer group leaders had, in fact, undertaken to schedule a second tour through France for me, spanning May and June. They left time open in the middle of this sixty-day period for me to attend a major pan-European ecumenical charismatic congress in Strasbourg. This event was to bring together Spirit-filled Christians from every part of the Body and from both eastern and western Europe.

It was during this second sojourn in France that I was to undergo many strong experiences with the Lord—and receive deeper understandings of what God's plan was for the ministry and my life.

18

Lion and lamb

The first weekend in May, which began my second tour through France, brought me to an unusual new charismatic religious community called The Lion of Juda and the Slain Lamb at Cordes, a stunning medieval town north-east of Toulouse. Arriving at Cordes I found monks, nuns, married

---

[31] See Acts 2.38–39, Proverbs 22.6, Matthew 6.7–11.

couples and their children and a number of single laypeople all sharing a contemplative lifestyle.[32] The complex of buildings itself was an old Capuchin[33] convent. Since 1975 it had been the mother-house of the community. The surroundings and the community's style of dress made me feel I had stepped back in time at least two hundred years. The warm welcome I received, however, soon made me feel at home.

Members of the community explained to me that it had been founded in France in May 1973 by a man now known simply as 'Ephraim', originally as a monastic experience for Protestants. Later, the community had become Catholic with the goal of being a centre for charismatic and contemplative life 'in the heart of the church'. From its earliest moments the community had felt itself called to reflect two aspects of Jesus in his life on earth—that of the vulnerable Lamb who is sacrificed for the sins of men and that of the powerful Lion who conquers the forces of evil.

Financial security, I was told, was renounced in favour of an abandonment to the Lord's providence: the community's constitution instructs them not to buy food for more than the week ahead. I identified strongly with this principle; in my own walk I had felt called to rely on Providence day by day.

Living by this principle the community had founded ten houses in just nine years, six in France, and houses in Israel, Italy (near Rome), Morocco and Zaïre.

The following week at the community's house at Nay, the Monastery of St Dominique, in south-west France, I was to meet Ephraim, the founder, and his wife, Jo. Both spoke English, as well as French and Hebrew. I learned that Ephraim was raised in the French Reformed Church of his parents, and became a pastor in that church. Then, after

---

[32] 'Contemplatives' in general are men or women living a consecrated religious life in monasteries or convents who devote a substantial portion of their daily lives to prayer, either privately or in community. Prayer times vary according to community, from four to perhaps six hours a day. [33] Capuchins are members of a 'reformed' branch of the Franciscan order established in 1525.

founding the Lion of Juda, he became Catholic and later was ordained a deacon.

I experienced a very strong anointing during my ministry to the community, which included praying for individual needs. Later, I jokingly asked Ephraim if the community would consider adopting me. He laughed. God, however, would take the 'joke' more seriously than either Ephraim or I did on that May afternoon.

On this same occasion I met Father Albert de Monleon, OP, a Dominican theologian, who served that day as my translater. In months to come this priest would generously give of his time to answer theological questions that I had as I developed my ministry in Europe.

Also at Nay I was invited to take part in a special time of prayer among shepherds (leaders) of various houses of the Lion of Juda who had come for that day. As I began to pray for these leaders the Lord gave a very strong prophetic anointing,[34] and I received a word of prophecy for each one.

During these sixty days in France I held some thirty different services from the Belgian border to the Mediterranean. Attendance at these meetings averaged around five hundred, considerably higher than I had been used to in the United States. The services in Bordeaux and Lille were ecumenical. In both places meetings were held, successively, in the Catholic church one evening and the Reformed church the next, or vice versa; the leaders of each group attended the service hosted by the other group. I began to see that God was asking me to minister to Catholics and Protestants brought together in one place, and to help them reach out to and pray for one another.

In Lille, on the second evening of ministry, I underwent a new and challenging experience: The service began, in a Dominican chapel, at 8.0 pm and continued, uninterrupted,

---

[34] In my own experience what I call a special 'prophetic anointing' occurs infrequently. It ushers in an abundance of prophetic words during a time of ministry; often these prophetic words are for a good number of different people present.

until 2.0 am, the first time I had ever ministered under an anointing of the Holy Spirit for as long as six hours. The next afternoon, while resting in my room, I felt terribly empty, as if I had given every ounce of myself the previous evening. I broke into weeping. 'Lord,' I asked, 'are you training me for endurance?' He was. From that point on services lasting from five to seven hours became the norm.

Many people expressed amazement over how I could minister for five, six or seven hours consecutively and still appear to have as much patience and compassion for the last person I would pray for as for the first; never appearing to tire, and never seeming to rush; always ministering to each person as long as was needed. During the period of prayer for individuals, the main concentration of myself and the whole team would be to keep our eyes on Jesus. We encouraged those present to continue in praise, prayer and adoration, similarly centring their attention on Jesus.

Often the Lord would bless us abundantly with a strong manifestation of his love and glory. In this atmosphere, while we were ministering under the anointing of the Holy Spirit, the team would feel sustained by a supernatural flow of strength.

Shortly after a service was over, the team would experience a return to feeling 'just normal,' and a natural tiredness would come upon us.

An evening in Bayonne turned out to be especially memorable. The local Catholic charismatic prayer group, with Philippe and Jill Maucorps as leaders, had planned to have me minister in their regular meeting room in a convent. As members spread the word, many more came that night than were anticipated. People soon jammed the room to overflowing and others sat or stood outside looking in through the windows. As soon as I walked into that solid mass of people I realised it would have been next to impossible to hold the service there. Someone suggested we all move outside into the convent's garden.

There was a flurry of people grabbing cushions, chairs and benches, and resettling themselves in the garden all around me, some even sitting on the ground. I thought briefly of Jesus being hemmed in by a throng as he stood by the lake at Genesaret.

Candles lit the garden and the air was perfectly still as the service got under way. 'Come, Holy Spirit,' I prayed. Suddenly there came a strong breeze that kept the candles flickering for a long minute, almost blowing them out. The breeze stopped as abruptly as it had come. But later in the meeting, as we contemplated Jesus' love together in stillness, the breeze rustled through the garden again, just as before. Both times the breeze brought us a special awareness of the Lord's presence by his Spirit.

As I went from place to place in France, the phenomenon of 'resting in the Spirit' occurred as it had in the United States. However, this was not considered 'normal' in Europe, and soon a very secondary phenomenon occurring in the Renewal became a focal point of controversy.[35] Some of the questions were: Just what was this phenomenon? Did suggestion play a role? Did this experience really incorporate a work of the Holy Spirit? Something else began to happen as well. As I would leave a place, the leaders in charge of a given community or prayer group would find that as they prayed for their brothers and sisters, resting in the Spirit would continue to occur. This did not happen in just one or two places on that second tour, but in many where I ministered. I had never seen this before. And it was not only 'resting in the Spirit' that continued to take place, but also an outpouring of the gifts of the Holy Spirit, such as prophecy and healing.

Others were as perplexed as I was. One theologian remarked to me, 'It seems as if this phenomenon of resting in the Spirit can be "transferred" from one person to another; what do you think?' But I didn't know what to think. My only recourse was to pray and ask that God would give me some understanding of what was happening, and why.

---

[35] See John Richards, *Resting in the Spirit*, Renewal Servicing, PO Box 366, Addlestone, Surrey, KT15, 3UL, UK and Philippe Madre, *Repos dans l'Esprit*, Pneumatique, Paris.

In response to my prayers I felt a definite 'No—it cannot be transferred.' It was also as if the Lord was reminding me of the request that had been made in prayer for me with the laying on of hands in 1980 in Tyler, Texas: that the Holy Spirit would be stirred in me and that God's power and anointing would be liberated strongly in my ministry. And how the day after, as I prayed for people, most of them experienced resting in the Spirit. I was also reminded of the fact that everywhere I had gone in France I had prayed for leaders, through the laying on of hands, the same prayer that had been prayed for me: that God would stir his Holy Spirit in them as never before and set free in the ministries of their communities his power, anointing and gifts.

It was also as if, in this time of prayer, the Holy Spirit reminded me of Paul's instruction to Timothy to remember to 'stir up the gift of God' (KJV) or 'fan into flames the gift of God' which Timothy received through Paul's laying hands on him.[36] 'The gift of God' is the Holy Spirit himself.[37] With prayer the Spirit in his power can be stirred in any community open to receive him.

Where people ardently desire to see the Holy Spirit work with great liberty, where the moving of the Spirit is not quenched, manifestations of his gifts and power will occur. Through whom, when and where these manifestations occur will be of the Spirit's own choosing. We do not, and cannot, command the Holy Spirit. He blows where he wills.[38]

19

Strasbourg

Before I knew it, Pentecost weekend and the major gathering of Christians at Strasbourg was almost upon me. Somehow I had had a notion, during my first visit to France, that a door would open for me to minister during this congress. When I

---

[36] See 2 Timothy 1.6.   [37] See Acts 1.4.   [38] See John 3.8.

then realised that that meeting would see 25,000 charismatic Christians from every part of the Body and virtually every country in both western and eastern Europe converge on Strasbourg, I told myself, 'Lord, that sure was a foolish thought I had.'

The night before I was to take the train from Pau to Strasbourg, however, I received a phone call telling me that my accommodation at the congress had been changed; I was going to be lodged with the leaders and the main speakers. Moreover, I would have a chance to participate in the workshop titled 'Exercising the gift of healing in the church'. The workshop dealt with the healing ministry of Jesus and how the church was rediscovering this ministry as a sign of Jesus' love for his people of all ages.

When I arrived I was invited into a spontaneous time of intercessory prayer by two men who were leaders in the Charismatic Renewal in France: Daniel Ange, a priest who had spent many years as a hermit in the deserts in Africa and France, and Pascal Pingault, founder of a community called Pain de Vie (Bread of Life), whose main outreach was to the poor and the marginalised. They had both felt powerful impulses to intercede for the congress about to open, and they asked me to join them.

'Let's just pray,' they said to me, and together we got down on our knees and asked God to pour out his Holy Spirit upon the gathering.

As we entered more deeply into prayer I was surprised to find that I had an inner vision. I found myself in a large circular room that was otherwise empty. Its walls, however, consisted of a series of doors, one right after another.

'What does this mean?' I implored the Lord.

The impression on my heart that I then received seemed to say: 'Behind those doors are the different parts of the Body of Christ.'

'Lord,' I exclaimed, 'are those doors going to open and are all the parts of your Body going to walk into the room and find themselves in a new oneness through you?' There was no answer. I persisted: 'Are the doors going to open this weekend? Is this congress the signal of a new beginning together for your church in Europe? A new unity?' But I heard nothing. All was silence.

The weekend was indescribable. I had never before been in so huge anassembly of charismatic Christians—and these were Europeans, a blend of so many cultures and so many different languages. I was one of very few Americans present. The congress drew much of its inspiration from the way God channelled his Spirit through the speakers, especially through David du Plessis and through Thomas Roberts, the venerable Welsh evangelist transplanted to France who had been inspired to convene the meeting.

Catholics, Protestants and Pentecostals attended sessions together, sang together, both in European tongues and in the Holy Spirit's own heavenly language, and sat side by side in the theme workshops. They also chatted at the bookstalls and over meals. When Thomas Roberts' talk concluded on an especially challenging note, the orchestra made up of both Protestant and Catholic musicians from many different lands responded with a rousing praise song. Many in the assembly broke into spontaneous dancing.

Another dramatic moment came when Sister Briege McKenna, a Catholic nun born in Northern Ireland, and a Protestant pastor from Northern Ireland who had been raised to hate Catholics but had let his heart be changed by the Spirit, stood on the main platform, arm in arm, and led the 25,000 in singing 'Father, make us one.'

We came together for many things that weekend, Protestants and Catholics sharing with and getting to know each other. But when time for communion services arrived, we had to separate. There were two celebrations, one for Catholics and one for Protestants. And a burden fell upon the people, a burden that I later came to believe God actually desired his people to feel. There was a painful awareness of the continuing divisions in Jesus' Body on earth—an awareness many at Strasbourg had probably never experienced before that weekend.

As I was entering the Protestant area to partake of the

Lord's Supper—to be held simultaneously with the Catholic Mass—a Catholic girl came up to me and said, 'I'm Catholic; will you forgive me for the divisions in the Body of Christ?' I looked into her eyes and said, 'I'm Protestant; will you forgive me?' Spontaneously we fell into each other's arms and embraced and wept together.

Similar scenes, perhaps with other words but with equally poignant meaning, were happening between thousands more at Strasbourg that weekend. God was issuing a call to repentance over the sins of the divisions of the past, divisions that separate us from our brothers and sisters in Christ and thus, at least in part, from the Lord. Only by embracing in his love, we were learning, would the unity of Christ's Body, so ardently desired by the Father, be accomplished.

The Catholic Mass at Strasbourg, I was later to learn, contained a very poignant moment: the beautiful chanting of a psalm by a Messianic Jew (a Hebrew Christian from Israel), Ruben Berger. The cantor had been invited by the liturgy team for the Mass to sing the psalm in Hebrew between the Old Testament and New Testament readings.

Before chanting the psalm, Ruben told the Catholics at the Congress: 'I lived in Galilee and I am neither Catholic nor Protestant, but a natural olive branch grafted back onto its own tree.' He added, 'I, like you, believe that in this eucharistic celebration we will be partaking of the body and the blood of Jesus.'

Even more than the gestures and symbols I have just described was involved in the painful process of repentance and reconciliation, however. Something quite unexpected. On the second day of the congress, a Sunday, I began to feel registered sharply on my heart the words, 'Daughter, come home! Come home!'

'Are you calling me home to Europe, Lord, to the land of my father and my mother?' I cried out. 'Are you calling me home to their spiritual roots in the Lutheran church?' I did not receive an answer. My spirit, however, felt so pierced that I began to weep and kept it up for perhaps twenty minutes. The next day, Pentecost Sunday, I felt the same impression, as strong as before, 'Daughter, come home! Come home!' Tears came again. Every effort on my part to hear some explanation of this call met with frustration. There was only silence.

Finally, on Monday, the last day of the congress, as the assembly packed into a football stadium together I heard again the inner call, now more urgent than ever: 'Daughter, come home! Come home!' I began to weep relentlessly. I would have gone anywhere the Lord had indicated to me, so overcome was my spirit. But I still could not learn where 'home' was.

I did receive some satisfaction, however, in understanding better the vision I had had while praying with Daniel Ange and Pascal Pingault. When I saw the stadium, the vision seemed to resume. Only this time the playing field before me took the place of the circular room.

'O God, it's still empty!' I said in my spirit.

An inner voice said, 'Look around you.' I did and saw that the stadium seats were completely packed, with more people standing and crowding tightly around the fence on all sides of the playing field.

'That's where my church is,' it seemed to me the Lord was saying, 'on the threshold of a new realisation of her unity —that my glory might cover this earth!'

20

Healing his Body

From Strasbourg on that Pentecost Monday I went with members of the Lion of Juda to their community's house in the Vosges mountains in eastern France. The house, Abbaye Notre Dame d'Autrey, had been established by Augustinian monks in the twelfth century and had often been rebuilt. The Lion of Juda community had only recently begun to live there.

Here I had a chance to speak with two messianic Jewish brothers, Ruben Berger, who had canted the psalm at the Strasbourg Mass, and his older brother, Benjamin. They had been at the large ecumenical congress through contacts with Ephraim's community in Jerusalem. They loved the Lord very much and had been living in Tiberias in Israel for the last twelve years.

Benjamin told me that his Austrian mother and his German father had fled Nazi terror separately in 1938 and had met in Antwerp, Belgium, where they had sought refuge. There they were married, then migrated to the United States. After he and his brother Ruben found Jesus, they responded to a call in their hearts to go to Israel and settle. The brothers nonetheless were marked by the Holocaust: their grandparents, aunts and uncles perished in the Auschwitz death camp.

At one point in our conversation I mentioned to Benjamin how painfully aware I had become of the divisions in the Body of Christ through my experiences at Strasbourg, especially the separate communion services.

'So many of us who love the Lord Jesus are yearning for the unity of his Body (his Bride),' Benjamin told me. 'But many are not aware of where the first break in the Body occurred and are also not aware of the identity of the olive tree onto which they have been grafted and into which we who are Jews have been regrafted. The original major break that took place was not between Protestants and Catholics, as most people believe, nor even between Catholics and Orthodox.

'The first break occurred shortly after the very beginning of church history and was between the gentile church and Israel: that Israel that had always had the messianic hope; that Israel which Paul describes as the natural olive tree.[39]

'To heal the torn Body of Christ,' he said, 'we must go back to the beginning; we must also understand that this healing will not be complete, the Body will not be whole,

---

[39] See Romans 11.

until the natural olive branch, the Jewish brethren, come back into their own inheritance (which is Jesus, the Messiah of Israel), and until the two, Jew and Gentile, become one new people through the reconciliation of his cross, the Messianic tree, producing together the good fruit—the fruit of Christ, filled with the oil of his anointing.'[40]

The community had a special service and a blessing of the house planned for that evening. They asked me to minister during the service.

Just as we entered into praise in the chapel, my spirit again resounded with the call, 'Daughter, come home! Come home!'

I broke into tears and wept and wept.

'Lord,' I pleaded through my tears, 'I've got to stand and minister in a minute! I can't go on crying like this!'

My gaze went up to a stained glass window in the chapel, a window depicting the Virgin Mary and Jesus, and the sun was just pouring through. As the light struck the windows, the answer came to me about the call to 'come home'. It was as if the Lord was saying to me, 'I'm calling you back to the bosom of Abraham, Isaac and Jacob; I'm calling you back to the depths of your spiritual home—back to Israel, your Jewish roots.'

I felt a transpiercing of my heart. In an instant, the Spirit took me back through the whole history of Christ's Body, bringing me into union and harmony with each part, a total oneness. No longer was I someone that could walk among the different denominations in an impersonal way but it was as if I had now become part of each part of the Body.

I had lived through one overwhelming experience after another in my four days at Strasbourg and Autrey. I could well have done with some rest after such events, but there were others in store just ahead.

Ten days after the Pentecost Monday celebration at Autrey, on June 11—the fourth anniversary of my surrendering my life to Jesus and the second anniversary of my call to

---

[40] See Galatians 3.26–29; 5.22–23.

full-time evangelistic service—I was holding an evening service at Versailles for the Catholic prayer group there. During the service I heard in my spirit three words that were to infuse my whole life with new and urgent meaning:

'UNITE MY CHURCH!'

Late that evening, alone in my room, I began to plead with God: 'Lord,' I said, 'I don't understand! Are you calling your church to come together by saying, "Unite, my church?" Are you calling me to take part in that process by telling me "Unite my church?" If so, Lord, I'm not qualified for such a task!' I was just starting to comprehend how complex the Body of Christ on earth had become.

For the moment I kept my counsel, not daring to share this impression with anyone. If this was of God, he would provide confirmation. I had, in any case, not the slightest notion of how to go about uniting his church. The idea was thoroughly intimidating.

My next stop was Chartres where I was to spend three days in intensive prayer in the upper room of a convent of Dominican sisters. There were five of us joining together in prayer, a Franciscan priest, a Dominican priest, the superior of the house and her assistant and myself.

At one point during our prayer I found my mind conceiving of the church as a tree, a very old and very large tree. As I thought about what makes up a big tree I recognised that its roots lie unseen underground, that its trunk is huge at the base and virtually unmoveable, and then, going higher, that it has branches of various sizes.

I came to perceive that the inter-denominational movement was like the tips of the newest branches. Coming back through church history, I could see that various other renewal or reform movements were the branches on the tree: the Pentecostal movement around 1900, the Wesleyan movement in the 1800s, the Baptist movement in the 1700s and the Lutheran and Calvinist Reformations in the 1500s. Even lower on the tree was the fork in the tree caused by the split between Constantinople (Greek Orthodox believers) and Rome in 1054. Finally, one gets down to the trunk itself—the Catholic[41] Church, and, not to be forgotten as my brothers from Tiberias had reminded me, the church's roots in the heart of Israel.

Through the late twentieth-century outpouring of his Spirit, known as the Charismatic Renewal, I also felt, God was sending new waves of power and revivification through *all* parts of the Body, from the leaves right down to the roots.

These reflections also led me into contemplating the notion of a 'family tree', a spiritual family tree: that God is my Father and Jesus is my brother, and therefore I am related to all who claim these same relationships.[42] As my three days in Chartres came to a close, it was suggested to me that I might want to visit Chartres Cathedral, one of the most splendid and storied churches in all of France. I readily agreed. Entering the church, however, the great architecture and the cathedral's works of art were not what commanded my interest. I felt a sudden and strong desire rise in my heart to go to the side altar consecrated to Mary.

Though the cathedral was immense I found myself walking straight to this place. I sat down and felt tears begin to pour from my eyes. For the first time in my life, faced with the reality of Mary, I was able to say 'Mother'. I could not fully understand everything that was happening inside of me, or why it was happening; but I knew what had begun was a healing in my heart and a new understanding of Mary's role in the church founded by her Son to last for all ages.

During our period of prayer in those three days, a prophetic word came forth from the Dominican mother superior: 'I give you a new name: Catherine Marie.' Since the word spoken bore witness in my heart, that is, I felt it came

---

[41] The word 'Catholic' comes from the Greek word meaning 'universal'. The word 'Protestant', by the way, derives from two Latin words—'*pro*', meaning 'for' or 'in favour of' and '*testari*', meaning 'testify to' or 'witness to'.

[42] See Romans 8.14–17; 29–30.

from the Holy Spirit, I began to use the name Kim Catherine-Marie Kollins.

The mother superior and her assistant also took the occasion to broaden my awareness of Saint Catherine of Siena. She was an Italian Dominican nun who had exercised her ministry by travelling all around Europe in the fourteenth century and by writing letters of encouragement or reproof to church leaders far and wide. One of her prime concerns had been the healing of a badly torn Christian body. Though she had very little education and indeed was unable to write in her own hand, necessitating dictation to a scribe, she became one of only two women ever named by the Vatican as 'Doctor of the Church' (the other being Theresa of Avila).[43]

While I listened I felt a strong emotional identification with this woman of six centuries earlier, and with her mission. It was then that it occurred to me that the day I arrived in France to begin my second tour, April 29, was her feast day.[44]

In this century, I was starting to see, my role in the Lord's calling of his church to unity was to share with others that which I had experienced myself. I was thereby to help brothers and sisters from one part of the Body understand those from other parts.

---

[43] 'Doctor of the Church' is a title bestowed by the Catholic Church on a theological personage posthumously to recognise an extremely high degree of spiritual insight into important doctrinal questions.

[44] In Catholic liturgical practices a 'feast day' is a day of remembrance of a saint, usually the date of the person's death.

21

Blending into Europe

The Dominican priest I met at Chartres was Father Michael Marsch, a theologian and psychotherapist from Germany. For the past two years he had been exercising a ministry combining his psychiatric training and his insights into prayer for healing at the therapeutic centre of St Luc near Toulouse in France, a house of the Lion of Juda. I was delighted to meet someone with connections in Germany, the European country in which my own family was rooted. 'Could you possibly open any doors for me to minister in the German-speaking countries?' I asked cautiously. Fr Marsch's reply at the time was something so vague it could not have been taken for a 'yes'—only a remote 'maybe'.

My next to last week in Europe on that tour, now in mid-June, was spent at the Lion of Juda house at Pont Saint Esprit in Provence, in the company of Ephraim and his wife, Jo. There I shed my American 'look' for a new sort of clothing. When I first came to France I looked *very* American: my hair was coloured lighter than my normal blonde; I used light touches of make-up, and I wore classic clothing such as a white suit with a purple blouse and medium-heeled shoes. It was a 'look' that was considered very acceptable for ministry in the United States. The only problem was it was not good for Europe.

As my second French tour proceeded, God began to change me. First the make-up went; now at Pont Saint Esprit, Ephraim asked me about the colours of clothes I wore. I told him that I now wore white when I was conducting a service, that is, ministering, and purple at other times. 'Aren't you always in ministry?' Ephraim asked. Suddenly I knew in my heart that from then on, I would wear only white. The community made me clothes that would serve better in a European ministry—a light cream dress made of Ethiopian cotton with a scarf to cover my hair, and leather sandals. At first I thought the head covering had to do with convenience —letting me handle my schedule without taking time for my hair. Then I came to see it was a way to let my hair grow out to its natural colour.

This was part of a process in my life that I came to call my 'onion experience'. Jesus has assured us that 'whoever would save his life will lose it, whoever will lose his life for my sake will find it'.[45] The more God took me through the process of dying to myself, the more I found myself come alive in Jesus. At one time I had been quite materialistic; I watched God separate me from my attachment to possessions and to lead me into a much simpler, less complicated life style. It was like a stripping, like the peeling of an onion. The Lord peeled off one layer at a time of my human attachments. Each time a layer came off I felt pain. At times I would feel very uneasy in my heart about what was happening to me. After every new layer had been peeled I would think, 'That's it; it's over!' God, however, would reveal to me that more of my outer 'skin' had to go, and there would be more peeling. Never was this in violation of my personal freedom, however; it always required my saying, 'Here I am, Lord; go ahead and peel me some more.'

Another thought started rising to the surface of my mind as I finished this tour: Was it possible that God was showing me that my place in the Body of Christ was in the Catholic Church? I discussed this thought with Ephraim as we strolled together through a vineyard. One point in particular that Ephraim made stayed in my thoughts—that a French bishop, a Franciscan, now shepherding a diocese in Morocco, a man sensitive to the moves of the Spirit, would soon return to France for a new assignment. I had just a fleeting thought, something like 'if I ever did take a step into the Catholic church, this bishop could receive me'. The bishop's name was Mgr Jean Chabbèrt.

The last week of my first prolonged stay in France, I took time to reflect on the differences between what I had

---

[45] See Matthew 16.25.

experienced in my ministry in the United States and in my ministry in Europe. The Europeans were frequently ready to show enthusiasm in worship, but always with a sense of decorum and propriety.

The Holy Spirit changed my style of praying for people. No longer did I know who, specifically, was to be prayed for; thus I could not ask individuals to come forward as before. Instead, I was simply led to extend an invitation to all who wished prayer to come forward. Rather than myself and one other person praying for each person's needs, I prayed with two others, forming a team of three. Now, too, I had to minister through a translator. This seemed to reduce my liberty to yield to the Holy Spirit in the prophetic gifts. The greatest blessing I saw from the new style of praying for people was that it was welcomed in different parts of the Body in Europe; Catholic, Protestant and Pentecostal.

I also felt that the intensity of anointing of the Holy Spirit on my ministry had increased since my coming to Europe. An anointing can often be perceived through the senses. From one service to another there can be significant changes in its intensity. When there is a strong anointing, the fruits of the ministry also appear to be more plentiful—conversions, reconciliations, healings, deliverance from evil influences, greater commitment to discipleship.[46]

There is no way to predict the moving of the Holy Spirit in a service, I have learned. He does not fit into our pre-established designs. The Holy Spirit is the unpredictable One *par excellence*, and we cannot control or manipulate him. The most we can do is simply be ready to receive and respond to his leadings.

And what, then, is the best way for leaders to prepare themselves for a service and open themselves to the Holy Spirit's guidance? From everything I believe the Spirit has taught me, I would say the following: Leaders should be reconciled among themselves, should pray for unity and, finally and most importantly, should love and serve the Lord

---

[46] Refer to p64 'Call to Ministry' (Section II).

Jesus as the service unfolds. ('Our first service,' I frequently tell leaders and music groups, 'is simply to love Jesus.') Then, at the outset of any assembly, leaders should encourage all those present to do these same things, too.

From another perspective, for the person who is ministering under an anointing, there comes a supernatural boldness to proclaim the Gospel. The spoken word springs to life and has power to penetrate into the hearts of those listening. I believe that what happened on the Day of Pentecost was that Peter was fired by this kind of boldness as he arose to speak to the throng in Jerusalem. When the people heard Peter's anointed message, 'they were cut to the heart' and three thousand were converted.[47]

Another change in the way the Holy Spirit worked through me as I ministered came in expressing the gifts of the word of knowledge and the word of wisdom. Whereas earlier I had received such words while I was praying for individuals, one by one, now the Spirit was manifesting these gifts through me in a new way (though continuing also in the first way). As I reserved a part of a service for waiting upon the Lord to see if he wished to bless us with his gifts, I would at times receive a word of knowledge or a word of wisdom impressed on my heart for individuals, or groups, present in the service. What I experienced was the same inward motion of the Holy Spirit in both manifestations of these gifts. Upon receiving the Spirit's leadings, I spoke the words out to the assembly.

During this trip I could see, looking back, that I had also grown in my appreciation of the various ways Christians from different parts of the Body understood and prayed for what I had always known as 'the Baptism in the Holy Spirit'. The church that had prayed for me to receive this experience believed that, in their words, 'the Baptism of the Holy Spirit is evidenced by speaking in tongues'. By this they meant that the person who had been prayed for was expected to start speaking in tongues as evidence of the reception of the 'baptism'.

---

[47] See Acts 2.37–41.

This is what I personally experienced that night in Orlando, Florida. And, as my ministry began, this was also my personal belief. During my first two years of ministry, when I laid hands on people and asked God to baptise them in the Holy Spirit, they also began praying in tongues. From my experience, I would have said this understanding was correct.

However, in Europe, in the midst of the traditional churches, I found that there were other theological understandings of this experience.[48] Among other things, according to these churches, the reception of the gift of tongues was not a necessary evidence or confirmation of a person's having received this 'baptism'. What was more, they referred to it by other names: variously, 'the infilling of the Spirit', 'the infusion of the Spirit', 'the release of the Spirit' and 'a new outpouring of the Spirit'.

Who was right—or wrong? Were there 'right' and 'wrong' understandings? I sought the Lord to understand how I should pray for people, and what name I should give to this experience while praying.

One afternoon I was ministering to a small group of people who wanted prayer for this experience. None of them spoke English. So I decided that, as I prayed for one after another, I would use different names for the experience I was asking God to give them. I used 'release', 'infilling', and 'outpouring' of the Holy Spirit. Each of them apparently received the same experience that I had. Some began to weep gently, while others were very still. Still others told of feeling great joy. All of them received the gift of tongues, and began to pray in their new tongues.

This encounter gave me a new confidence that it was the Lord who saw the desires in each heart. It did not seem to matter which of the names I used in praying for this experience. What mattered was that Jesus saw the desire in each heart to receive of his Spirit, and he responded to that desire. After that, wherever I would go, and no matter what part of the Body I would be ministering in, I deliberately chose to

---

[48] See Sullivan, *Charisms and Charismatic Renewal*, pp59–75.

use the name for this experience which that part of the Body was accustomed to using.

On other occasions in Europe I met Christians who told me that they had been baptised in the Holy Spirit, which was very obvious to me, but had not begun to speak in tongues, though they desired to. (Even though some of them had been used in other gifts of the Holy Spirit, such as prophecy.) I simply prayed with them that they would receive the gift of tongues—and they did.

In ways such as these I gained insights into some of the conflicts, often sharp, that arise in the Charismatic Renewal over questions of how the Holy Spirit moves in our midst. Had I stopped with my early approaches to experiences in praying for the 'Baptism in the Holy Spirit', I would have concluded that *that* way of praying was *the* way. However, God is much bigger than our experiences.

There is even some humour in all this. In France, as, in future days, in other countries that were new to me, it would typically take me a few days for my ear to learn to distinguish a foreign language from tongues. I would have to ask my translator, 'Is that person speaking in tongues? Or is he just saying words in his own language?'

Before leaving France for my home in Dallas, I asked Patrick Grace to schedule an autumn tour of Europe for me and especially to see, through Fr Michael Marsch, if meetings could be arranged in Germany, Austria or in German-speaking Switzerland. Early in July Patrick phoned him and relayed my request. Michael quite blankly told Patrick that it was impossible to arrange anything at that time of year.

'Everybody will be on vacation now,' he explained on the telephone, 'and, besides, if the Germans have one charism for sure, it's the charism of organisation—everything will be planned at least until the end of the year.'

Patrick told Michael that even if he could manage just two or three invitations, I would be delighted to come and minister. The Dominican priest concluded the conversation by saying he couldn't promise anything.

22

Discipleship

That same July, in 1982, while I was leading a service in Texas and as praise was beginning to rise from the assembly, I found tears starting and I could not stop them from flowing. Such tears are not like normal crying out of sadness or out of joy; the tears just start unprovoked by an emotion. In this instance I felt led to open my Bible and my eyes fell upon Mark 10, where Jesus says, 'Verily, I say unto you, There is no man that hath left house, or brethren, or sisters, or father, or mother, or wife, for my sake, and the gospel's, but he shall receive a hundredfold now in this time, houses, and brethren, and sisters, and mothers, and children, and lands, with persecutions, and in the world to come eternal life ' (Mark 10.20–30, KJV).

The hour had come, I felt God was showing me, to give up my home. And to leave my country and my children behind.

As the call came all sorts of emotions were released inside of me. I entertained the thought, 'What if I never have another home, what are you going to do then, Kim? What will the children do if they have no place to come home to, to call a home?' But as the tears flowed, they appeared to wash away all the reservations in my heart. My younger son Darin was already living with his father in Florida and my older son Robert would be moving out from my house soon to attend Bible college. As for myself I would leave for the Middle East, Africa and Europe in early September, not knowing how long I would be gone. The most difficult thing left to deal with was that we had two dogs that we loved dearly; I wondered how we would find a loving atmosphere for them in somebody else's home. If God had made all these arrangements, however, I finally concluded, couldn't he also find a substitute home for our beloved dogs? Wasn't every detail accounted for in the Father's master plan?

I did not know what was going to happen to me, except

that very soon I would be on a plane heading for Israel to walk the land that Jesus had walked, then off to Morocco and Europe for ministry. But the Lord was certainly teaching me how to let go of people and things that were dear and walk as a disciple.

When the rich man comes to Jesus and says, 'How can I be a disciple?' Jesus tells him to sell all he has and follow him.[49] The young man's unwillingness to do this is very sad. The problem is not that the man is rich but rather that his riches hinder him from becoming a disciple. Nothing must block our response to God's invitation into his plan for our life, whatever that is. And we shall find that the more things we abandon, the freer we shall become—and the more radically dependent on the Lord.

It took a month to close the house. Many things we simply gave away. We put some things in storage and allocated some to Robert to take with him to Bible college.

We had many difficulties during this period of transition. At one point I arrived home from a tour of ministry in South Carolina and found that the house had been broken into and many valuable things had been stolen. Finally, the day came when the move was complete. It was just a day before my son's departure for Bible college and a few days before my embarking on the flight for Israel.

Robert had just enough money to pay his tuition and set up his living quarters at the school, and for his last night in Dallas he planned to stay overnight with his cousins. On the way to his cousins' house he had trouble with the air conditioning unit on his car and pulled off the road to see if he could find the trouble. He had the car's bonnet open and was inspecting the unit, when a car drove up behind him and stopped.

'Need any help?' he heard a voice behind him say. He sensed that there were two individuals standing behind him, possibly more.

A moment later Robert felt a knife at his throat. His assailant (or assailants) cut him in the neck three times, but

---

[49] See Matthew 19.16–24.

not very deeply, then knocked him out and rolled him into a ditch. When Robert regained consciousness he found that all his money for Bible college had been taken, and his glasses were broken.

About 4.30 am Robert dragged himself up to the front door of the house where I was staying with friends. As he came in and explained to us what had happened to him, I felt a holy anger[50] rise up inside of me.

'Satan, you are the defeated enemy!' I exclaimed. 'You can try to mount your various attacks upon us but you are still defeated!' I said this even though Robert's money was gone and we could see no way for him to follow through on his plans for starting Bible college.

Within four days Christian brothers and sisters from my church, International Christian Centre, contributed enough money to replace everything Robert had lost in the attack, and he left for Bible college as planned.

The house given up, Robert off to college and suitable homes found for our dogs, I boarded a plane in Dallas for Tel Aviv. With me I had one suitcase and two carry-on bags containing little more than two cotton dresses, a couple of blouses, a sweater and sleepware, and just forty dollars in cash. In Israel I was to be met by members of the Lion of Juda and lodge at their house in Jerusalem.

Once in Israel I very quickly came into contact with two different people with material needs. Following what I perceived as impulses from the Holy Spirit I gave twenty dollars to the first person, then twenty to the second. That left me with no money at all. I reviewed the passage about Jesus sending off the seventy-two disciples and telling them to 'Take no money', and something resonated very deep in my heart. If I needed even small change to make a phone call from an airport I would have to trust the Lord to supply it on the spot. I felt my dependency upon him very keenly.

---

[50] 'Holy anger' is a term often employed in the inter-denominational Charismatic Renewal. On at least one occasion Jesus manifested such an anger. See John 2.14–16.

God was teaching me about walking in discipleship. I began more and more to let go of material things—more of 'the onion experience'. I had once earned an executive salary and was accustomed to 'the good things of life'; it was quite an experience to see this 'letting go' occur. I watched God strip me of possessions—jewellery, clothes, house.

Then I watched the Lord begin to strip my heart of things that weren't supposed to be there, wrong attitudes, prejudices, false understandings. It was just a start, to prepare me for my next steps along the road with my Lord . . .

I also saw him moving me far away from my country. That had meant quite an internal struggle, but then I felt an impulse that the next two years would be like 'being away at school'. This thought settled my spirit.

I also had a deep inner sense that somehow Robert and Darin would be able to fly to Israel and spend Christmas with me in Bethlehem. I could not imagine how this would happen. Even though my own schedule called for me to return to Israel for Christmas, I had no funds available to fly my sons there.

By faith, however, I wrote to both of my sons, told them of my hopes and asked them to apply for passports.

In Israel I found a special fulfilment of the Lord's call to me, 'Daughter, come home! Come home!' Among the Jewish people I started to identify my spiritual roots. I also carried forth the calling of the Body to unity in Jesus as I ministered in widely diverse Christian communities in and around Jerusalem: with the Jewish brothers, Benjamin and Ruben, at Tiberias; the English-speaking Protestant prayer group; a Benedictine monastery, and the house of the Lion of Juda. (In Israel, and certain other countries, the community goes under the second part of its name, calling itself the Community of the Slain Lamb.)

From Jerusalem I flew to Morocco for ten days of ministry to the Lion of Juda house there and my first experience of visiting a predominantly Muslim country. Claude Brenti, the shepherd of the house, and his wife, Cathy, were waiting for me.

Shortly after arriving in Morocco I felt that the Holy Spirit was leading me to undertake a three-day fast. As I started my fast I also felt it was urgent that I read my Bible. Once I picked it up I felt that I would not be able to put it down. First I read the Acts of the Apostles. Then, as I was reading the introduction to the Letters of St Paul in the Jerusalem Bible, I came across notes on the order in which certain scholars think Paul wrote his epistles. I decided to read them in that order. This process gave me new insights into the progressive understandings that Paul and the others received through the Holy Spirit's enlightenment. I began to see how what was lived and experienced in Christian communities under the Holy Spirit's guidance became part of what was then written down as a guide for present and future generations. This exercise helped me to appreciate the development and positive worth of Christian tradition.

Once back in Europe, I immediately called Patrick Grace to see what, if anything, had been planned for the German-speaking countries. I learned that Father Michael Marsch, OP, had scheduled me for a sweeping 33-day tour across Germany, Austria and Switzerland. 'When Michael tells you how this tour all came about,' Patrick assured me, 'you are really going to be amazed.' He also told me that Michael Marsch had decided to accompany me on this tour; this would be the first time I was to have an interpreter on a regular basis and help me with meeting people and with all the sundry arrangements of an entire tour.

Before the planned stops in the German-speaking countries, however, I was scheduled for eleven days of ministry to a variety of Catholic and ecumenical groups in France. This tour started at St Leu in Paris, where a parish-based charismatic community is anchored by a group of Dominican nuns. I spent a day seeing people individually for counselling and prayer, then the next day shared preaching and leading of the weekly charismatic prayer meeting with a priest named Raymond Halter.

The leaders of the Pain de Vie (Bread of Life) community picked me up at St Leu and drove me to their house in

Sommervieu in Normandy; this assembly of about forty adults and forty children shared a life of holding to the elemental necessities in the spirit of the early Christian communities. In a special chapel in their house the Holy Sacrament is exposed twenty-four hours a day. As I walked into their chapel I was struck by a powerful presence of the Lord. Kneeling, I entered into silent prayer. Almost an hour later, though I realised it was time for me to go to another activity, I found it almost impossible to get up and leave, so captivating was the manifestation there of God's glory.

At my next stop, in St Broladre in Brittany, the newest foundation of the Lion of Juda, as the first bursts of wintry cold began to blow through the stone corridors, I came to realise that my light cotton dresses were no longer adequate clothing.

I had come to Europe without anything to wear in winter. The Lord, however, had assured me that he would provide. Ephraim's wife Jo and I were trying to figure out together how I could quickly be provided with some protection against the cold. There were no stores nearby where we could obtain material to make clothes. As we walked into the community's sewing room I spotted several large bolts of light beige and white wool material laid aside for the making of drapery. 'That will do!' I told Jo. I thought for a second and then described to my hostess with gestures how I felt the material should be cut and sewn. Next day, when I left, I was warmly clothed in an outfit that included a cape, and on my next visit to that house I matched the drapes on the community's windows!

Finally, at the Chemin Neuf (New Road) community in Lyons, where Catholics and Protestants share a common life, I held a two-day workshop for the leaders on the healing ministry of Christ. I visited the community's centre for discipleship training and spoke to seventy people of all ages who were attending the current course.

During Chemin Neuf's weekly prayer meeting, I gave a teaching on faith expounding on Hebrews 11, with about four hundred people present. This chapter contains my favourite verse on faith: 'Now faith is the substance of things hoped for, and the evidence of things not yet seen' (Hebrews 11.1, KJV). Perhaps the hardest line in this passage for some Christians to receive is the teaching that 'without faith, it is impossible to please God' (v. 6). All too many of us like to consider ourselves committed, fervent Christians because we read God's Word and gather regularly in worship. All the same we may never really risk exercising our faith; we refuse to step out of the boat of our worldly security systems and walk on the water toward the Lord, trusting him for all things.

Throughout my stay in Lyons I was battling against a severe cold and sore throat. In between ministry appointments I was constantly going back to bed to rest, take medication and sip hot tea. All the while my host community kept up intercessory prayers for my recovery.

On my fourth and last day in Lyons, my cold now somewhat abated, I found myself getting excited with anticipation about what was to begin on the next day: my tour into the German-speaking countries. Fr Michael Marsch was to meet me at Chemin Neuf in the morning and we would drive to Hochheim, West Germany, for our first scheduled stop. I was eager to learn, too, how the tour came about—and what stops we would make.

23

Into Germany

The next day Michael arrived at 9.0 am and we got under way for a tour that would encompass thirty-three days and ten cities.

In the car Michael told me that the way the tour had come into being was really extraordinary. He recalled how he had told Patrick Grace by phone that he did not think much could be arranged because of the German tendency to plan meetings so far ahead. 'On the way from the phone back to my room,' Michael related, 'I had an inner vision. It dealt with the gospel reading that we heard in the Dominican convent at Chartres. It described Jesus' telling the disciples that on their way to Jerusalem they would meet a man in the streets and they were to tell him that they wanted to celebrate Passover in the "upper room". And the upper room would be all prepared.

'By this vision I was sure that your trip to Germany, Austria and Switzerland had already been prepared by the Lord. We just had to find the means to step into the Lord's preparations. So in about half an hour I wrote a two-page letter recounting my observations of your ministry and you. In order to get two or three invitations I figured I'd need to send out about twenty letters to friends, and this is what I did.

'Instead of receiving two or three invitations for you to minister, I received thirty-five!'

I was truly surprised to see how the road ahead of me had been paved. What happened was that those who received copies of Michael's letter passed them along to friends and acquaintances. A half hour at the typewriter turned into a schedule that would keep me busy for the rest of 1982 and well into 1983.

Most startling of all was the invitation with which I was to begin my tour in Germany: Michael had sent the letter to a Catholic couple in Hamburg. They passed it to an associate of Pastor Wolfram Kopfermann, the co-ordinator of the German Lutheran Charismatic Renewal. When the man saw the signature on the letter he exclaimed, 'I know this person (Michael Marsch)! I was in school with him in Jerusalem.' Thus he showed the letter to Pastor Kopfermann, and a decision was made to invite me to speak to the National Lutheran Charismatic Congress.

Instead of the invitations coming, as they did in France, for local and regional meetings, the order had changed. 'Lord,' I prayed when I heard the news, 'you didn't have to start me with a national-level meeting in a new country, a new culture and a new language.' I was frankly overwhelmed. I had no idea how my ministry would be received.

Then I bombarded Michael with questions. 'Tell me all you can about German culture, about the history and the present state of the churches in Germany, about the Charismatic Renewal in your country,' I said. He began to answer my various questions. Shortly, I interrupted him with what later came to be called 'Kim's famous question'. 'What is the difference,' I wanted to know, 'between Germany and France?'

Michael laughed and laughed. Finally he said, 'Germany and France are not only different countries, they are different planets!' As the months and years ahead rolled by I would learn just how naïve that question had been. How little most Americans know about Europe and the diversity of its various cultures. When I was in business travelling to Europe I would stay at very good hotels and deal with high-level executives and never really get to live with the people. In my ministry in Europe I had to die to many of my American notions and expectations and open up to receive the beauty and diversity of Europe's peoples. That the Germans are highly organised and that the French are given to deep, logical thought patterns (known as 'Cartesian thinking' after the mathematician and philosopher René Descartes); that the Swiss are very reserved and conservative in their lifestyles . . . these are all perhaps stereotypes. But these generalisations do contain a lot of truth and must be experienced first-hand by a visitor to be appreciated.

En route Michael and I pulled off at a rest stop on the autobahn in West Germany. There I discovered something that Americans would find highly curious: the rest stop included an 'autobahn church'. Michael asked if I would like to go into the chapel and pray, which we did. Afterwards, over food in the adjacent restaurant, Michael produced an astonishing letter from the Bishop of Bali, Indonesia. The letter was in response to one of the letters Michael had sent off about my ministry.

WHERE IS HOME?

He had come across an address of a Swiss nun he had known years before; she was now living in Indonesia. He decided to write her a personal letter and, half in jest, included a copy of his letter about me, adding a handwritten postscript, 'Why don't you invite her too?' What he did not know was that this nun had become secretary to the Bishop of Bali. Who would have guessed that she would show the letter to the bishop—and that he would extend to Michael and me an invitation to come to Indonesia? That, however, is what was contained in the letter that he was showing me.

We arrived in Hochheim, not far from Frankfurt, for the National Lutheran Charismatic Congress on a Thursday night, with the congress already into its second day. Originally I was scheduled to hold a workshop of ninety minutes on Friday afternoon parallel to other workshops. The theme I spoke on dealt with healing: how the healing of any individual in the Body contributes to the healing of the whole Body of Christ. When they learned of the theme, it was decided to cancel the other sessions; this meant that the whole congress was able to come to my workshop, about five hundred participants.

In my sharing, translated by Michael Marsch, I laid great emphasis on forgiveness of others as an essential part of the healing process, both for the healing of individuals and for the healing of the torn and wounded Body of Christ.

The impression among the leaders grew that they should dedicate the evening to prayer in connection with this theme. That evening we had a time of praise and prayer, including prayer for individuals by laying on of hands from 8.0 pm until midnight. Up to that point only some of those who desired such prayer had received it, so the congress leadership decided that the next evening's service should be a continuation of the night before.

Back in my room after the last evening's service, I reflected over what had happened. Instead of doing our ninety-minute workshop as originally scheduled, we had a workshop and two evening prayer services, one lasting four hours, the second lasting five hours.

That was already quite a lot. More important than that, however, was a deep understanding I received of Jesus as the Lamb of God. During the Hochheim congress, I found myself again in the midst of controversy regarding the phenomenon of 'resting in the Spirit'. The controversy was brought about primarily by one of the guest speakers, who challenged the validity of this experience. The result was confusion among the various leaders.

I had been preaching a message of reconciliation and unity, and it appeared that the fruits of disunity were being manifested. Because of this controversy I found myself in a position where I felt I was almost like a lamb being led to slaughter. In that moment I caught a glimpse of Jesus as the innocent lamb being led to slaughter to redeem the sins of the world. (Ever since that point I have retained a strong identification with Jesus as the Lamb of God. As soon as I enter a new chapel or church the first thing I look for is a depiction of a lamb, either a stained-glass window or a bas-relief or a painting or a symbol on a banner. I inevitably experience a great leap of joy in my heart when I find one.)

After the closing service of the congress the following day, many people came up to Michael and me to comment on the evident unity between us. They were struck by the unity in two people who came from such different backgrounds, cultural, spiritual, theological, denominational. I realised through their comments what an unusual thing the Lord had done in sending us out together, a Protestant woman evangelist from the United States and a German Dominican priest.

Michael and I had planned to leave Hochheim about noon that day, which was a Sunday, but we were invited for coffee by a Lutheran evangelist named Gunter Oppermann and his team of young people. Gunter and the young people, roughly half of them Lutheran, and half Catholic, worked together in a youth evangelistic and outreach ministry called Projektion-J ('Project' and 'J' for 'Jesus'). They would travel by invitation to different churches throughout Germany, whether the churches inviting them were Lutheran, Catholic, or 'Free church' (every other denomination, including Baptists, Methodists and Pentecostals), preaching conversion and discipleship.

Instead of simply having coffee with them we ended up praying with them for several hours. Much later Gunter admitted to me that he was the only one on the Lutheran charismatic co-ordinating committee who had opposed inviting me to speak at the Congress. He had personally had too many negative experiences with American evangelists trying to 'save Europe'. Gunter and his team also reported later that their ministry, from the day of our visit, took on new vibrancy: transformed, they said, by a fresh infusion of God's power and love. They found that the number of people attending their services doubled and the number of people coming forward to give their lives to Jesus increased greatly.

From Hochheim we went to the Black Forest to a tiny spot in southern Germany almost at the Swiss border. There we visited a Protestant charismatic healing community organised in households. Families who were members accepted into their homes disturbed people to let these people receive healing through therapeutic conversations and prayer and sharing of the families' lives. Here we had five days of very hard work. Even though the community was small, we had to minister to individuals and to families in intensive counselling and prayer. This turned out to be as draining as it had been to minister to the entire National Lutheran Charismatic Congress in Hochheim.

24

Zurich

We next crossed the border into Switzerland, another new culture. We drove to Kappel, one hour from Zurich, where an evening of ministry was scheduled in a Protestant retreat centre called the House of Stillness. The house was under the leadership of a Reformed Church pastor. Thirty to forty people were expected to gather for the evening.

Here the Lord taught me much about stillness. My experiences in worship thus far had been primarily with spontaneous prayer, joyous praise and adoration in groups. Try as we would, Michael and I found great difficulty in encouraging these people to enter into the kind of praise that I had been used to. For one thing there was no music and praise team. I started to say to myself, 'This isn't going to work.' However, what this community and its guests were accustomed to were long periods of deeply anointed silence. And in the midst of those silences God moved mightily and touched many—much to my own surprise.

What I learned through this evening was that God can work through virtually any human expression of emotion, from clamorous shouts of praise to total silences, and that we limit God whenever we insist upon imposing one form or another of praise on people who may have had very different experiences of worship from our own. Ministry demands not routine repetitions of our previous experiences of praise and worship but great openness to the Spirit's move for each particular group and each new gathering of the Lord's people.

On the following morning Michael and I met with the elders' council of the German-speaking Swiss Catholic Charismatic Renewal. Having received Michael's letter about my ministry, they wanted to become personally acquainted with me. We spent several hours with them discussing various aspects of my ministry in Europe, and ended with lunch.

On Sunday afternoon in Zurich came our third and final event in Switzerland—a meeting organised by a Free Church lay person in a school auditorium with invitations to members of charismatic prayer groups and their guests. The organisers expected 100 to 150 people for a service of praise and a sharing of God's Word and closing with a period of prayer for individuals by laying on of hands. They called the evening 'a blessing service'.

We had told our hosts that for this type of service we would need teams of people to help to lead music and praise, to support the entire service in prayer, to usher, to counsel people, if needed, after they had received individual prayer. People chosen by the leader for these various services came to a session at 2.0 pm in which Michael and I tried to give them as much guidance as possible for the evening's events. To get such teams into the proper state of readiness when no one from the local group has had any previous experience with this type of service is not easy. Especially when you must do the training through translation, or rely on someone else to do the training for you.

The afternoon service, scheduled for 4.0 pm, was not, despite our preparations, to go as smoothly as we had hoped. There were many surprises in store, not all of them easy to accept.

Upon arriving at the auditorium I had a notion we might have trouble handling the flow of people coming and going. It had been planned that we would conduct the service not from the stage but from the auditorium floor. Because there was only one exit door in use, and that at the front right side of the auditorium, people entering or leaving would have to cut across the front, possibly interrupting the ministry.

At 3.30 from backstage I glanced through the curtain into the auditorium and saw that the place was almost full and people were still streaming in. It was clear that many times the number that we had expected were already present, not 100 or 150 but more like 650.

I returned to the team of people interceding for the meeting backstage and we intensified our prayer. Roughly at this point I experienced a poignant flash of memory, recalling my first visit to Zurich in 1971 as a young business executive. I suddenly found myself in tears as I realised that it was here in this city that I received a phone call from my father telling me that my mother had fallen critically ill, and then had lapsed into a coma, and asking me to get home quickly. Coming back to the present, twelve years later, I felt my sadness being replaced by a surge of joy as I reflected that I would soon share on the theme of the call to reconciliation and healing of the divided and torn body of Christ.

But where was the music group? It was almost time for the service to begin and they had not yet arrived. The musicians, however, were not local; they were coming from southern Germany, and had simply been delayed. Thus, the meeting had to start late. Backstage, we continued in prayer.

When the meeting finally did get under way, the time of worship and praise and then teachings by Fr Michael Marsch and myself seemed to go well. Then came the moment for prayer with individuals. When the invitation was extended, instead of people coming up in the orderly way that we had planned, they massed together and jammed to the front, then stood in rows five or six deep. Meanwhile, others who did not plan to stay for this time of prayer were crossing this same area to exit. To say the least, there was a lot of confusion.

To compound our difficulties some members of the teams that we had prepared disappeared. I asked Michael what had happened to them. He looked at his watch, saw that it was now six o'clock and told me. 'It's supper time in Switzerland; they've probably gone somewhere to eat.' And that indeed was what had happened.

With the return of the missing team members from their supper, things seemed to improve, but at 8.30, still very much in the midst of our prayer ministry, we ran into another obstacle. A man appeared who said he was in charge of the premises and that it was time to lock up the building.

We announced the situation to the assembly, even though there were over a hundred people still waiting their turn for prayer.

Immediately a solution presented itself to us in the form of a man who was the caretaker of a Methodist church. He told us that his pastor had been in our service all afternoon and that the pastor was inviting us to take everybody to the Methodist Church and complete the service.

So, in an ecumenical pilgrimage, we left the auditorium and went through the city of Zurich to the Methodist church, where we continued the service for another ninety minutes. What a day! Six and a half hours of service, not always under ideal conditions. But through it all, the name of Jesus was lifted up and glorified.

Exhausted, we returned to the House of Stillness, looking forward to a full day of rest on the morrow. The day was very precious. I even had time to catch up on the notes I had been keeping on this journey. I wished the rest could have been prolonged several more days, but this was not to be.

One recollection from Kappel that remains especially strong is of a fourteen-year-old boy with long hair and sideburns who attended the service in Zurich and listened intently to every word spoken. The following day this boy tried to get in touch with me and Michael Marsch all afternoon, but could not find us. So he gave an envelope containing 250 Swiss francs to our host as a love offering for our ministry. In an attached note the boy said that he had worked hard all summer to buy a motorbike but that when he heard our sharing about what God was doing in Germany, France and the United States, he decided to turn all his savings over to be used for the Lord's work.

The Holy Spirit had touched this boy's heart very deeply, and Michael and I, in our turn, were deeply touched by his sacrifice.

No sooner had I begun to get accustomed to Switzerland than it was time to leave and drive to Austria. Again I found myself bursting with questions about another new country and its history and culture. I tried to glean from Michael's answers all the information I possibly could to prepare me to minister to another people.

We had been invited to Innsbruck by a Catholic prayer group and the service was to be held in the parish church of St Norbert's. The news of the Zurich meeting, we found, had preceded us to Innsbruck and people were already concerned that similar confusion might take place. However all aspects of the service unfolded in a very disciplined and harmonious fashion. This despite the fact that once again the attendance came as a surprise. Though 100 had been expected, some 450 appeared for the night. Interest was so keen that a second night of ministry was added and another 200 people came.

25

Berlin

The tour was now half over. I had experienced three countries in two weeks. Now, over the second two weeks, the tour would have me weave back and forth between Austria, Switzerland and Germany. My stops included Vienna, Altstatten in Switzerland and Lindau, Munich, Kaufering, Saarbrucken, Hamburg and Berlin in Germany.

The spiritual highlight of the tour for me came in one of the meetings in Berlin in a large inter-denominational church. Gathered for an all-day Saturday meeting were some eight hundred Christians of many different churches, including Catholics, Lutherans, Baptists, Methodists and Pentecostals. Their numbers included many priests and pastors.

Fr Michael Marsch and I shared the duties of providing the teachings for the day.

Michael introduced our teaching programme by telling the assembly: 'We don't have a programme, and you don't have a programme. What we hope is that God has a programme.'

God did. First of all, he showered down upon the whole gathering the strongest anointing of the Holy Spirit I had yet experienced in my ministry in Germany. As our praise mounted higher and higher, a real oneness developed in the assembly. Then I found myself totally caught up in a powerful prophetic message. It was almost like becoming a tempest erupting with the Lord's burden for his people, the members of his still very torn and divided Body on earth.

I want to share with you a part of my teaching at that hour in Berlin and the prophetic utterances that were woven in;

they are important moments in my journey with the Lord and, I feel, strong words for Christians in pilgrimage toward unity.

'My prayer is that the gift of God be stirred in you as never before,' I told the Berlin assembly. 'The desire of the Spirit all over this world is to be loosed to bring the Body of Christ into perfection for the return of God's Son. I cannot emphasise enough that Kim Kollins is nothing special at all. It was the time and the hour for the Spirit of God to move, and I have been used as nothing more than a vessel to water seed that the Spirit had already planted.

'All the glory and the honour and the praise go to our Lord.

'When we come together to praise, we are lifting up our glorious Saviour. We are putting forward our faith believing that he will take the promise of his Word to the performance of his Word.

'Praise God that his kingdom is at hand! Oh, what lies before us! We cannot even completely comprehend it. But Jesus is calling us to be his disciples now, to give everything we have, as we have never given before. If you've decided to follow Jesus and give him everything, I want you to sing out not to the world or the one next to you, but I want you to sing out from your heart that decision unto the Lord.'

We all launched into singing the chorus of 'I have decided to follow Jesus.' I then continued:

'For two years God has spoken these words to my heart, "It is only the beginning." At first I thought he was referring to me and to the ministry he gave me, but no, that was not it. It's a word to the Body of Christ. It is only the beginning of what we have seen from our Lord.

'We will see the fullness of his glory and I believe even greater than what was manifested in the first church will be manifested in our midst.

'In division the Spirit cannot move, but as the Spirit is uniting his church it is opening the way for power and glory to flow from God. God is restoring the fullness of his church. And I thank him.'

At this point I felt a prophetic word rising up and I spoke it forth: *'And know ye not that I am faithful to perform my Word, saith God. And have I not said that I would imbue you with power? Know ye not that ye are my temple and ye are filled with my precious Spirit? And yea I shall ignite the flame of the Holy Spirit within you this day as you have never experienced. But know as the flame of the Spirit burns brightly, it will consume those things in you which are not of me. But reach out today and receive by faith that which I have spoken unto you . . .*

'We stand here today for his entire Body all over the world,' I resumed. 'And I would like every priest and every pastor that is here to come forward. Thank you, Jesus. And God would speak this to you. He has brought you to labour in this divided city that is a symbol of his divided and torn Body. As you unite in prayers for the reuniting of Berlin and of Germany, God is going to put a burning desire within you to reach out and pray for the reuniting of the Body of Christ, because this city will be a symbol to the world of the unity of his Body.

'Yea, saith God, I have called you to lead my people. And know that my anointing, my hand, is upon each of you. Lift up the work to which I have placed your hand this day that I might bring it forth in the freshness and the fullness of my power. Reach out this day unto me, and know that it is only the beginning of that which I will do within this city. And it will be like throwing a pebble into a brook, that the ripples will go forth in an ever-widening circle that will be larger and larger and larger and larger. It will be a sign unto this world that IT IS IN UNITY THAT I CALL MY BODY! United in the blood of Jesus Christ of Nazareth, brothers and sisters in Jesus, each a member of his precious Body, each with his own position in the Body . . .'

Spontaneously I began to sing a solo song in English: 'The blood that Jesus shed for me, way back on Calvary; it's the blood that gives me strength from day to day, and it will never lose its power . . . It reaches to the highest mountain, and it flows to the lowest valley. It's the blood that gives me strength from day to day, and it will never lose its power.'

Caught up in the Spirit's flow, I forgot to wait for translation and continued in English, 'The blood of Jesus has set us free. And it's through that blood that we are united today; and oh, how I thank the Lord for the precious presence of his Holy Spirit and for the anointing and the power of his Spirit this day upon our lives.

'I thank the Lord for the stirring of his Spirit that we will never be the same, but that we will go in a new dimension of his power and his glory, that we will not be concerned with self but that we will focus our eyes upon him in a new way, and that we will truly answer his call to discipleship, that we will walk in the power that he gave us as he died upon the cross for our sins . . .'

I then went into the final part of the prophecy, which, staying in the powerful flow I had been experiencing, I again gave without waiting for translation:

'Unite, my church; unite, my church, saith God. Unite as one, that the banner of Christ might be held high before this world, for only through him can you enter the sheepfold that is the kingdom of God. Unite! Unite! And wave the banner proclaiming that he is risen, that he is alive! That he is coming for his bride, that he is coming for a spotless and blemish-free church. Unite! Unite under the banner of Jesus Christ of Nazareth, and march forth as soldiers of the army of Jesus Christ, proclaiming the gospel of Jesus throughout this land. Unite! Unite! Unite and prepare to move under the banner, held high, the banner of Jesus Christ!'

Not until five years later, while I was listening to a tape of this Berlin service to gather material for this book, did I realise that there had been no translation of the last prophetic words; only participants who knew English had been able to follow. As I listened to the tape I felt again the intensity of that moment. I also had a sense that the Lord was asking that the message of Berlin no longer be confined to the few who had understood it that day, rather that it be transmitted, exactly as it occurred, to all who read this book.

26

Roots

The last stop on my first German tour came in Hamburg, a weekend meeting organised by the Lutheran Charismatic Renewal. This stop brought me close to my mother's birthplace of Buxtehude. A leader from the meeting who lived in Buxtehude invited me to drive there with him. He found the street where my grandparents had lived—Kirchenstrasse; I saw the large Lutheran church at its end, the church where my mother had been baptised. I walked the cobbled street next to the wall against which I had played ball as a child, across from my grandparents' house. The house itself, the wall, the cobblestones, the church . . . everything was the same. Afterwards we drove to the outdoor swimming pool where I had spent many wonderful afternoons. All this evoked fond recollections and put me in touch with part of my childhood.

Then, last of all, we went to the cemetery to look for my family's burial plot. It took me twenty minutes of inspecting gravestones before I came upon the name 'Bellmann'. There were the names of my grandparents, two uncles and an aunt. My family roots . . . !

On the drive back to France, I reflected on my amazing journey of the last thirty-three days. The intensity had been almost more than I could handle. There had been sixteen major meetings that had lasted an average of five hours each, and twenty-eight meetings with leaders, and I had come into contact with some ten thousand people. I was worn out but joyous, and in that state of happy exhaustion, I kept hearing the words resound over and over in my heart, 'It is only the beginning . . .'

I also realised then, more dramatically than I ever had before, that my life was no longer my own, that it was given over to service, to be where the Lord wanted me to be and to serve however, wherever and whoever he chose.

We are all called to serve. Some are called to stay right where they are, others to go to another land. It does not matter what we are called to do, because one service or work of evangelisation or charity is not more important than another in the Lord's eyes. What matters is that we do whatever God asks of us, from sweeping floors to preaching the gospel, in a spirit of humility, obedience and joy. The Body of Christ has many different members with a tremendous variety of functions, and *all* those members and functions are important to God.[51]

It is also, I believe, very important that we just be ourselves—doing things out of our own God-given personality and using the talents he has bestowed on us, not trying to be somebody we are not. We should each let the Holy Spirit work in us to bring out the deepest and best parts of ourselves. If we try to copy somebody else's approach or style, we probably will fail very quickly. In my first service I tried to piece together bits of another minister's words so that I would have an abundance of good material. It did not work at all. I found out that I simply had to be myself, and trust the Holy Spirit, or my preaching would not be effective. Sharing the gospel should flow out of a heart reflection on one's own experiences with the Lord; it should allow the Spirit to draw from oneself words anointed with power to penetrate the hearts of the listeners.

Ahead of me now I had another challenging month of ministry scheduled in France. This period basically went well but included my second car accident since the ministry began. I was riding in south-east France with two members of the Lion of Juda, sitting next to the driver. A hard object flew through the air and crashed into the front windscreen on the passenger side, sending shards of glass right into my face. Incredibly, I was not cut. Moments later, shaken by the impact, the whole windscreen shattered into thousands of pieces, rendering the car undriveable.

---

[51] See 1 Corinthians 12.12–27.

On the pleasanter side of memories from that tour in France was Thursday November 25. I had a wonderful Thanksgiving Day dinner in an old, charmingly restored house on a hilltop near Pau. Jean-François and Annie de St Denis, whose house it was, and other leaders of the Pau prayer group, invited me to celebrate this traditional American holiday, virtually unknown in France, so that I would not feel so homesick.

The brief tour in France ended in mid-December with an interlude at the motherhouse of the Lion of Juda, at Cordes. Talking with Ephraim on that occasion I reminded him of my request of seven months earlier 'to be adopted by the community'. This time Ephraim did not laugh; rather he took immediate action. As it happened my visit to Cordes coincided with the profession of monastic vows of poverty, chastity and obedience by about twenty community members. The then-bishop of Albi, Mgr Robert Coffy, received the profession of vows. At the same time a number of married couples and single lay people were given wooden crosses to wear on a leather thong around the neck as a token of their entrance into the community. Ephraim arranged for me to be part of the ceremony and to be given a community cross as a sign of my 'adoption' (even though I was not Catholic and the community statutes did not provide for any such adoption). It made me feel very privileged.

After the ceremony Ephraim presented me to the bishop whose name he had cited to me in our talk of seven months before: Mgr Chabbert. He had been aware of my ministry for some time, as he had been a bishop in Morocco during my visit to Casablanca.

By now I had been separated from my two sons for a longer period than I had ever endured before. God had called me not only to give up my home but to give up geographic closeness to my sons as well. In my heart, however, was a promise I felt I had received from the Lord—that if I was obedient in following him, he would give me good time with my children. It was not necessarily that I would have quantity time, rather that our periods together would be 'quality time', time to enable us to live deeper relationships as a family than ever before.

Just three weeks before the departure date that I had planned for my sons, the Lord touched somebody's heart to purchase round-trip plane tickets for both of them so that they could spend Christmas with their mother in the Holy Land. Thus we had three wonderful weeks together, staying in a flat in Jerusalem maintained by the Lion of Juda and exploring together the sites of Jesus' ministry, death and resurrection.

On Christmas Day we journeyed together from Jerusalem to Bethlehem to celebrate the birth of our Lord. It was the first long family trip we had ever been on together.

Also during this, my second visit to Israel, I met Thomas Roberts, the man who had had the vision to convene the Strasbourg Congress for Pentecost 1982, at the community of the Lion of Juda. He shared with me his preparations there in Jerusalem for an ecumenical conference to be held in that city over Pentecost 1984. I told him about my work for reconciliation, healing and unity in the church, and he listened intently. He expressed surprise over how many doors had already swung open to receive my ministry and he encouraged me to walk faithfully in that call. This greatly touched me because I knew how tirelessly Thomas Roberts had laboured for this cause and I sensed that in my own generation I was being called by the Lord to walk that same road.

27

Lessons in Zaïre—and elsewhere

Looking back over the autumn I found that the Lord had taken me into six countries: Israel, Morocco, France, Germany, Switzerland and Austria. What would the new year bring? I could only guess that the intensity of my ministry probably would not abate. Even now I was getting ready to leave for a seventh country, Zaïre. Ephraim wanted me to visit and minister in as many houses of his community as possible, even the most far-flung. That meant a trip by plane into the depths of Africa, and a rugged 100-mile overland drive by jeep to Kabinda, Zaïre, where the Lion of Juda staffs a bush hospital.

I had originally planned to fly from Israel to Zaïre; however, to obtain vaccinations and a visa I had to return to France. Once back in Paris I was told over the phone by the Zairean embassy that I could not get a visa because I was not French but American. Would this trip to Zaïre have to be routed via Washington? I paused to pray for guidance, then it came to me that I should go to the Zairean embassy and speak personally to the counsul. After hearing my story the consul authorised a visa to be issued.

I next went by train to Ordgen in southern France to join members of the Lion of Juda from Zaïre who were in the process of returning to their mission after time back in France. We flew from Nice to Kinshasa, the capital of Zaïre. Possibly as a reaction to vaccination against yellow fever, I was sick through most of the seven-hour flight.

After we arrived in Kinshasa, my companions told me that the easy part of the journey was behind me. Two days later we were to take another plane to M'Bujimayi, not a jet this time but a propeller plane whose times of departure no one was ever sure of; the plane was capable of being late by anything from a couple of hours to a couple of days. We continually had to keep checking at the airport to see when the plane would leave.

Even when we finally got to M'Bujimayi, the hardest part of the journey still lay ahead of us. A jeep was waiting to carry us through the bush to Kabinda, where the community's house and the bush hospital were located. The roads were impossible, crude and pocked with huge holes. The terrain was so rough it took us six hours in the jeep to go a mere hundred miles.

The return trip was even more complicated. The passenger plane never did arrive at M'Bujimayi and after two futile days of waiting, we secured seats on a cargo plane for the flight back to Kinshasa.

With all the hardships the trip to Zaïre was one of the most blessed experiences I had ever had.

Soon after my arrival in Kabinda I had the opportunity to be present at the births of two children in the bush hospital. As labour became far advanced during the first birth, a nurse asked if I would like to do the delivery under her supervision. Very surprised to be invited to usher in a baby, I quickly said yes. As the process continued, though, I became a bit intimidated and drew back, turning the birth over to the nurse. When it came time to deliver the second baby I decided to stay with the process until the end. It was quite a scene because a monk from the community was standing next to me translating instructions for delivering a baby from French into English and there I was as the midwife!

Two beautiful baby girls came into the world that day under my eyes, and one of them in my own hands.

The first birth was a first child for the mother and hence a more laborious experience; it took longer and was evidently more painful. The second birth was a second child for that mother and a much quicker and easier experience.

While in Zaïre I had the chance to visit two convents of nuns, and to pray in both places for the outpouring of God's Spirit upon the sisters.

In one convent I had not had time to speak with the Mother Superior before holding a service in the chapel. We went through the whole service and I found myself holding back on issuing an invitation for the sisters to receive prayer for a new outpouring of the Holy Spirit. After all, I told myself, I haven't talked this over with the superior. Following the service I went and sought her out.

'During the service,' I said to her, 'I had a strong impression on my heart that God wanted me to invite those who wished to be prayed for for the outpouring of the Holy Spirit to come forward. Could you please tell me: did I understand the leading of the Holy Spirit correctly or did I not?'

'You did,' she responded.

'In that case is there any possibility we could ask all the sisters to come back into the chapel so we could pray for those who wish to receive this experience?'

'Yes,' she said, 'Let's do that.'

So all the sisters filed back into the chapel and, glory to God, every one of them was open to receive what the Holy Spirit had to offer each of them. All together that night we joined in praising the Lord in other tongues. It turned out that the only person in that convent who had previously experienced this particular grace from the Holy Spirit had been the Mother Superior herself.

Two nights later I went through a similar experience in the second convent, where God poured out his Spirit abundantly. In the second community however there did not seem to be quite the same liberty and spontaneous joy. The outpouring of the Spirit in the sisters' midst was more laborious.

Reflecting upon what I had just witnessed in the hospital, I was led to compare the two births of baby girls to the births of the charismatic experience in the two convents. I saw that in the first convent there had been an extraordinary readiness to enter into praise after the outpouring of the Spirit. In the second convent it had not been the same; there was more hesitancy.

The Lord however appeared to be telling me not to compare the two experiences. Both were births, both brought new life into being. The important thing was that both 'children' were now alive; I was not to focus on the processes of birth.

One evening in Kabinda I took part in an intensive time of worship in the Lion of Juda chapel. A strong anointing fell on our gathering that night, as we sang the community's vespers service in French. We prolonged our time of praise beyond the usual period for vespers, singing songs of thanksgiving to a guitar. Toward 9.0 pm we decided to stop and leave the chapel. We went outside into a warm African night bursting with stars, but the anointing followed and soon drew us back into the chapel. A spirit of dance descended on us and we found ourselves dancing around the altar as David had danced before the Lord.

Finally, we left the chapel again. As community members and I were walking across the house's courtyard, I stopped suddenly and began to prophesy. The words that ushered from my lips told of how the Lord was going to do a marvellous work in Zaïre and how he would use the community as a lighthouse to radiate his glory to all of Africa.

My time in Zaïre flew by too quickly; I would have loved to have stayed longer. But by the end of January 1983 I was back in Europe to resume my ministry in the German-speaking countries. Now I was to fulfil additional engagements that had sprung from Fr Michael Marsch's two-page letter and to return to some places I had visited in the previous autumn. Invitations were divided between Catholic, Lutheran and 'Free church', and a curious thing began to happen. In most places where I preached or taught, the assembly would be ecumenical and, no matter which part of the Body was organising the meeting, participants would turn out to be roughly one third Catholic, one third Lutheran and one third Free church.

God was drawing his Body together, urging forgiveness and reconciliation as prerequisites for healing and unity.

During February a week's trip to Rome had been scheduled; I was to visit a house of the Lion of Juda at Monastère San Silvestro in the cool Alban hills south-west of Rome. However, weariness began to overtake me. Always before this, when I was either exhausted or sick, I could still minister standing in the Lord's anointing and letting his power supersede my weakness. I had never even missed a meeting where I was scheduled to minister. But this time my strength failed me. Soon after I arrived at the Italian house I was put to bed and had to stay there for all but one day of my visit. On that day, with members of the community, I visited St Peter's Basilica, and that same evening I ministered during the community's vespers.

Staying in the same Lion of Juda house on this occasion was Thomas Roberts. What a blessing it was to sit and listen to him again as he continued to relate his dreams and visions for the healing of the divided Body of Christ. I was so taken by the way he seemed bathed in the love of God, and I felt that the Holy Spirit had created a special bond between us.

On the flight back from Rome to Frankfurt I found myself counting the days before I would return to the States for my first visit to my country after living overseas for six months —and for a time of long-awaited rest. I had set aside the entire month of March for the visit. But there was a strangeness to this forthcoming trip, too: it would be my first time going 'home' but without a home to go to.

At the same time I was pondering in my heart the question of whether, in my own particular case, God was not inviting me to step into a different place in his Body for his own specific purposes. That place was the Roman Catholic church.

Ten days later I stepped off an intercontinental flight at the Dallas-Fort Worth Airport. I was back in familiar territory. However, almost immediately after my arrival I came in contact with a well-meaning person who was working actively to draw people out of the Roman Catholic church. He put into my hands two anti-Catholic books, which I proceeded to read. One book was so poorly researched and written it lacked credibility. The other book, however, appeared to me more solid; it sharply questioned certain Catholic doctrines and practices. I came to no conclusive understanding at the time, but the anti-Catholic books did remind me about the books I had read several years earlier condemning the Charismatic Renewal. In that first instance, I was already deeply involved in the Charismatic Renewal and knew from first-hand experience that the books' arguments were shallow at best and, in some cases, totally false. Now I thanked God for having had me experience the Catholic faith in Europe in languages I could not understand —obliging me to understand solely through my heart— before I was faced with the anti-Catholic books.

When I visited my pastor and I shared with him my ponderings about possibly stepping into the Catholic church, Marvin Crow told me: 'Kim, you must follow the path that God has prepared for you and be true unto the Lord, wherever that path may lead you in his Body. And know that I stand behind that which God has called you to do.' I waited for some confirmation about whether I was to enter the Catholic church, but none came. From time to time during my ministry I would have the thought in my head, 'Am I meant to be Catholic?' But it was also a time when I kept running into anti-Catholic material, in Europe as well as in the United States; so I decided simply to focus on living one day at a time and not spend energy worrying over this decision. If I needed to make that kind of change, God would have to show me very clearly; I would not make such a change on my own.

I returned to Germany on April 4, just days before my first scheduled meeting of a spring tour. This time Gunter Oppermann and his team from Projektion-J would accompany me for meetings in the German-speaking countries.

With Gunter driving me and two team members to the second meeting on our schedule on April 8, a terrible accident occurred. We were driving on the Landstrasse (a secondary road) to Viernheim when our car was struck head-on at 100 km an hour by a car driven by a man who had been drinking. The man could not stop as a car in front of him began to turn right. His car veered left, crossed the median and smashed into our car.

Both vehicles were Mercedes, and both were totally destroyed. It was a wonder that no one was killed, so completely had both cars been wrecked.

Miraculously, no one in either car was gravely injured. Another person and I were taken to a hospital for treatment of our injuries and released after three days. I sustained a large haematoma to my left arm and another injury to my spine from the impact of a person in the back seat being thrown forward and over my left shoulder. Gunter Oppermann actually went on to the meeting that evening where he and I had been scheduled to minister. Bandaged and leaning on a crutch, Gunter preached the love of Jesus for over an hour to a meeting of two hundred people.

28

'Father, make us one'

This accident could clearly have spelled severe injury or death for all of us. It came, I believe, as an attack by the enemy especially aimed at preventing me from experiencing what I did ten days later—on April 18—in the cathedral at Worms.

The Catholic prayer group of that city had invited us to hold a service in a side chapel of the cathedral. As Gunter Oppermann and I met with the leaders in a preparatory session, a Dominican nun asked me, 'Do you know what day this is?' I told her I did not; to me it was just another day.

'It is April 18,' she said. 'It was on this day and in this city that Martin Luther made his final declaration before the Diet of Worms, his famous speech with the line "*Hier steh ich; ich kann nicht anders!*" ("Here I stand; I cannot do otherwise!"). That declaration in effect began the Protestant Reformation.'

What is more, we were then in the year marking the five-hundredth anniversary of Luther's birth. The moment was charged with drama.

Entering the cathedral for the service that evening I found

myself surrounded by an ecumenical team, standing together in a side chapel, with about 120 people gathered for worship. The Spirit's leading was to pray for unity, and thus we began to sing out to the Lord:

> Father, make us one,
> Father, make us one
> That the world may know
> You have sent the Son,
> Father, make us one.

Something unique happened to the light in that chapel as our song mounted into the air. There was a transcendence of atmosphere, as if heaven itself were breaking through into our midst. A powerful anointing descended on our gathering and I received a very strong prophetic word, a word that was not just for me on that night or just for the 120 gathered in the chapel but a word that I believe God is speaking to the entire Body of Christ throughout the world.

'Just as I sent Haggai forth to proclaim that now was the hour to rebuild the temple, so I send you forth to proclaim that now is the hour to rebuild my church!'[52]

As this prophetic word concluded, the glory of God veritably ignited around us in that sanctuary. I knew then that that night was not like just any night. Something for which the Spirit of God had been groaning for over four hundred years had just been prophesied over our own generation.

After the service ended, an English-speaking woman who had just happened to come into the church as a tourist, had seen our gathering and had decided to join us, came up to me. I never did learn what denomination she was from but she told me:

'I have prayed for *years* for that which I saw happen here tonight!'

Details, meanwhile, arrived from Indonesia about the astonishing invitation that Michael Marsch and I had received

---

[52] See Haggai 1.

from the Bishop of Bali to come and minister in his diocese. Through the office of that bishop the original invitation was expanded to include scheduled stops in many other parts of Indonesia. We would begin our ministry at the national leaders conference for the Catholic Charismatic Renewal of Indonesia, and then travel to other cities in that country for additional ministry.

Toward the end of my April schedule with Projektion-J, my son Robert, having just finished his first year of Bible college with very high grades, came to travel with me for a month. He wanted some first-hand experience of the churches in Europe, and to see what his mother's ministry was now like.

In Reichenau, Austria, during a weekend of ministry with Youth With A Mission, God sent a powerful healing of the bruises Robert and I suffered in our relationship. One evening, very late, after a service, Robert had waited up late to talk with me; he had many things on his heart. He began to tell me about emotional wounds that he felt he had been carrying since childhood, many of which I perceived I had caused. Suddenly, I felt the Holy Spirit moving in my heart and prompting me to ask Robert to forgive me for my mistakes as a mother. He, however, had to struggle with this for awhile before he could finally say, 'Mom, I forgive you.'

One more experience in this season of ministry stands out sharply in my memory: I was asked to lead three evening services in mid-June for a group of black American service-men and their families stationed at a US base in central Germany. The group, which was inter-denominational, had the use of a German Lutheran church once a week for their services.

The first evening as we entered into praise and worship, I thought, 'O Lord, how am I going to be able to minister here?' Their way of expressing praise was so much more exuberant than what I had grown used to in Europe. I had become quite conservative in my style of ministry in order to blend into European cultures and expectations.

I need not have worried. No sooner had I opened my

mouth than God filled it with the kinds of expressions of praise and preaching typical of spirit-filled black Christians in the States. Nor did I find that I was having to push myself to flow into their expression of faith; it came naturally, effortlessly. I was really one with them.

When I arrived at my room that night I felt surprised over what had happened to me, and over what I had actually experienced in my heart. I was even a bit ill at ease that I had undergone such a radical, and sudden, change of style.

During my second night of ministering I went through the very same transformation of feelings and expressions. It was then that I recalled what I had come to understand in the piercing of my heart on Pentecost Monday at L'Abbaye Notre Dame d'Autrey: no more was I part of just one part of Christ's body, but, through a mysterious grace, I had become part of each different part. The Spirit was showing me that he could change me to adapt to very different worship styles—and that that adaptation could feel not artificial or forced, but natural.

29

Indonesia

Before I encountered a new country and culture I typically tried to learn as much about the place as I could. Thus, in trying to prepare for my time in Indonesia, I discovered that that country had the fifth largest population in the world —about 147 million people. I also saw that it was ninety per cent Muslim, five per cent Protestant, three per cent Catholic and two per cent Hindu, Buddhist and other. Soon after Fr Michael Marsch and I arrived in Djakarta, I saw that in Indonesia the very new shares space with the very old. Cars, for example, ride on streets filled with rickshaws and oxen. I discovered a whole new culture and received a startling awareness of the vastness of God's creation. None of my reading, in any case, prepared me for what I found in the people themselves. They exuded a friendliness, a humbleness of spirit and a gentleness to a degree that I had never seen anywhere else. Instead of one person greeting you at the airport, for example, there might be ten or fifteen people.

As in Germany, God had me start my ministry in this new country with a national-level meeting. In Malang, on the Island of Java, some 350 leaders had gathered for Indonesia's third leaders conference of the Catholic Charismatic Renewal, and there the Lord had me share many of the experiences I had had in ecumenical meetings, such as the congress at Strasbourg. The main message was a call for healing and unity in the Body of Christ.

Following this conference, Michael Marsch and I were informed of our schedule for the next thirty-two days. It embraced ten cities on three islands, Java, Bali and Sumatra, taking in six thousand miles of travel within the country. We then met with our prospective hosts, who were all attending the national conference. With the Bishop's secretary, Sister Jacinta of Switzerland, we set off on a five-week tour of ministry.

The Catholic Charismatic Renewal in Indonesia was young but dynamic and growing fast. In the areas we visited the renewal was usually only three or four years old, except for Jakarta, where it was seven. Indonesia's bishops had just issued a favourable evaluation of the movement and guidelines for its future development. During our own tour, in fact, we were received into the residences of five bishops, to whom we related our evangelistic travels. Father L. Sugiri, SJ, the co-ordinator of the renewal in Jakarta, hosted our last service in his parish church. The meeting counted 1,500 and seemed to me especially notable for its joy. What a great sight it was to look out over the throng and see all those hands raised to glorify the Lord.

My fondest memory however, is of the choruses of the Indonesian people's charismatic songs and the accompanying gestures, especially their version of 'His Banner over me is Love.' The Indonesian word for 'thank you', too, was beautiful to hear—'*Terima Kasih*'.

As the ministry expanded further and further and the distances became greater, I had to learn to keep things in balance. It is extremely difficult for me, for instance, to cross time zones. In my trip to Indonesia or my trips to the United States, I have found it takes me seven or eight days before I am sleeping normally in the new time zone. Though such frequent and long-distance travel has never been a desire of my own heart, I find that God has given me a considerable grace to bear up under such travel. It is only through this grace that I am able to continue to lead the kind of life he has called me to.

Along with the grace for travel the Lord has given me complementary graces to allow me to adjust to a variety of cultures, all quite different one from another, and to deal with Christian leaders and others so often through the medium of translation. Indeed, there have been many times when I had to lodge in someone's home with no translator present, and we had to communicate solely through gestures. Love, however, overcomes all barriers, and the love that comes straight from God through a relationship abandoned to his perfect will is the most powerful kind of all.

While I was ministering I had to adjust to another facet of my evangelistic calling: translation. To try to minister under an anointing through a translator, I have found, can be extremely difficult. There has to be a sheer unity between the one preaching or teaching and the person who is translating. If either the translator or myself is not responding to the Holy Spirit attentively, the whole ministry is weakened and the message loses its penetrating power.

Another difficulty I have had is learning when to tell people 'no'—'no, I cannot come'; 'no, I'm not able to provide this or that service for you'; 'no, I cannot pray with everybody here; the Spirit can work just as well through someone else.' The demands put upon a travelling evangelist at times become overwhelming. Unfortunately, my answer cannot always be yes to every request; much as it has been painful for me to learn, sometimes I have had to say no.

30

Ways of loving

When I returned to Europe from Indonesia I was able to spend a week in fasting and silence in a Lutheran community in Gnadenthal, Germany. The community gave me a room apart where I could be totally alone with the Lord. While here I went into ardent interceding before the Lord for him to bring my ministry into greater purity and holiness. What I wanted was to become more and more transparent so that his love and glory might shine more brightly through everything I was called to do.

During this period the Holy Spirit impressed more deeply upon me that we should have but one motivation for everything that we do: to love our Lord. To read and heed God's written Word, because we love him. To forgive others, because we love him. To walk the path that He has given us, because we love him. Whether we are living in obedience to someone he has placed over us, serving brothers and sisters in physical or spiritual need, or just doing the evening's dishes, our sole motivation should be the love we have for our Lord.

From Gnadenthal I travelled to Ars in eastern France, the home of the celebrated 'Curé d'Ars', Jean-Marie Vianney, where three French communities had joined together to organise a week-long meeting under the theme 'For God a Celebrating People!' I had been invited to minister there by the communities organising the gathering of five thousand: Chemin Neuf, The Lion of Juda, and Pain de Vie. Once again I would cross paths with that grand old gentleman of evangelism, Thomas Roberts, now in his early eighties and still agile and dynamic. During a very intense time of repentance and reconciliation among various leaders across denominational lines, I asked myself: were we, perhaps, ready to embrace each other in the God kind of love, not, that is, expecting the other person to change?

The Charismatic Renewal had a very special current of grace from the Holy Spirit, I had already realised. Reflecting back on the history of the renewal, I noted that this outpouring of grace had not been confined to only one part of the Body of Christ, but had flowed, and was still flowing, into all parts. This wave of the Holy Spirit had begun to break over Protestant areas of the Body in the 1950s and early sixties. It flowed into the Catholic Church in 1967. Gradually, through a common experience in the Holy Spirit, people were being drawn together in fellowship from different parts of the Body, many for the first time. People were coming out from behind their denominational walls; unexpectedly, they began to see Jesus in those from other churches.

The early 1970s was a time of great excitement, I knew from others' recollections, because many were trying to understand what the Holy Spirit was doing. People were approaching each other across denominational lines in a new openness and love. The love expressed, however, was often shallow. In some quarters comments such as the following could be heard, 'The traditional churches now have the Holy Spirit and they will leave their traditions and become like us.' 'Catholic charismatics will soon see the role of Mary differently and forsake their errors.'

People were embracing each other in a conditional love, waiting for others to change and become like them.

With the dawning of the 1980s, these expectations of change were not being fulfilled. Moreover, many Catholics and traditional Protestants were finding new life ignited by the Holy Spirit within the practices of their own churches, posing difficult questions for others in the Charismatic Renewal. Wasn't the Holy Spirit's promise to lead us 'into all truth'?[53] When then, if ever, would other charismatics correct their ideas? People who were asking such questions, of course, often understood their own ideas and ways as *the* truth.

As I looked around me at Ars, I found myself asking some

---

[53] See John 16.12.

very different questions: Is the first phase behind us now: that phase in which the Lord brought us together in such surprising ways and yet in which we often embraced in a conditional love? Is the Lord perhaps challenging us now to forsake our limited love and enter into a second phase in which we will embrace one another in our differences, without expecting the other to become like us?

A ten-week autumn tour that year, 1983, again with Gunter Oppermann and his ecumenical outreach team, took me to twenty-four cities between Germany, Austria and Switzerland, which allowed me to minister in fifty-two meetings. In Stuttgart, on a Sunday afternoon, we had a special surprise as we arrived to minister to the local Catholic prayer group: the Bishop of Bali, Mgr. Vitalis Djebarus, had come to join us in the service. The Indonesian bishop had been in Germany on church business, found out about our schedule and had come to see us. As we prayed for people's individual needs, the bishop joined in our prayers and blessed each person who came forward. How God loves to bring his children together for reunions, even across great distances.

I flew back to the United States on November 3 for a prolonged stay of three months. By now I was acclimatised to living in Europe; being back in the States meant passing through a degree of culture shock. In Europe, I realised, the pace was often slower, the cars smaller, the food tastier and more nutritious. Europeans were willing to take more time with things; fast food had not yet taken over the culture. In America many people were in such a hurry to go places, to eat, to 'get things done', epitomised by such things as certain supermarkets staying open twenty-four hours a day, seven days a week. What, as an American, I had once perceived as convenient now struck me as frivolous and unnecessary at best, unhealthy at worst. Having said that, however, I should add that I will always thoroughly love my native country, and I still appreciate many of its virtues, such as tolerance, friendliness and generosity.

To fulfil a promise I had made to my son Darin, I went to Orlando, Florida, for two weeks. By this time he had been living with his father, his stepmother and his half-sister for over two years. (And Darin would remain with his Dad until he graduated from high school.) He had adjusted well, was earning good grades and starring in his school's football team. Even though our separation as mother and son had been hard for both of us, I knew that it was important for a teenage boy to have a father close at hand. God had given me a deep peace in my heart about this arrangement.

An important event in Darin's life, one which he had been looking forward to, was parents' night in his senior year. This was a night dedicated to the parents of graduating seniors in the football team; it included a game and a half-time ceremony of the senior players and their parents being presented to the crowd. Some eighteen months earlier I had promised Darin that when that night came, I would be there. And so I was, cheering his team on to their victory.

My other son Robert, meanwhile, had been selected by his classmates as president of the student outreach ministry[54] at his Bible college. By phone Robert, bursting with excitement, told me about outreach projects that he and his Bible college class had undertaken, such as evangelising on the streets of Houston and ministering at local churches.

After leaving Orlando, I attended the International Women's Aglow[55] conference in Washington, and then undertook a month of ministry in the States, returning to some of the places where I had led services before going overseas. I ministered near Greenville, South Carolina, at a Pentecostal Holiness church, then was invited to appear on a Christian television programme there, recounting what I had seen the Lord doing in Europe, the ways in which he had been drawing his body together. My next stop was the

---

[54] 'Outreach ministry' in the United States typically describes a mission of sending people out from their church to evangelise or provide charitable services to people in surrounding areas.

[55] An international, interdenominational fellowship of charismatic women who come together once a month in local chapters for praise, prayer and sharing of testimonies.

Beulah Retreat Centre in central North Carolina for another week of ministry and a happy reunion with Ken and Rosali Edwards and their community.

My sons Robert and Darin joined me to visit my father for Christmas in Crescent City, Florida. We had a wonderful time together as a family in a small fishing cabin on the St John's River in Florida. I spent several more days taking care of my father. His health was failing. I joyfully plunged into cleaning his house, doing his laundry, cooking and undertaking other chores that he was no longer capable of handling. As on other occasions, I found that while God had certainly reduced the *quantity* of time I could spend with my family, he had improved the *quality* of that time.

Returning to Orlando, I found that the couple who had led me to the Charismatic Teaching Centre on that unforgettable night of June 11, 1978, where the Lord brought me back to him, were going through a hard time. They were having to move from their house because of various difficulties. In the process of moving, the wife had hurt her back and become unable to lift anything.

The Lord spoke to my heart and said, 'Go and serve them.[56] Go and clean the house that they are leaving.' And that is what I did, and I have never had so much fun scrubbing floors and washing walls. All day long, for four days, I was at their service to do whatever they needed done. Though I loved the couple dearly, I also felt that my service was unto the Lord; in serving them, I was serving him.

'God,' I prayed out of the midst of my labour, 'don't ever take away these kinds of graces from me!' I had such an incredible joy as I worked.

After the holidays I flew to Dallas to share with my home community, the International Christian Centre, in Garland. People there were excited for me about how so many doors had opened for my ministry in Europe and how warmly I had been received in seven countries. I told them that their prayers of intercession had certainly played a part in my

---

[56] See Galatians 5.13 and 1 Peter 14.

ministry's development. Here, as elsewhere in my travels, I emphasised how important it was to be open to receive all Christian brothers and sisters in the love of the Lord, no matter what their church membership might be. They prayed for me and blessed me with laying on of hands to send me back to the Lord's vineyard in Europe.

This indeed was the spirit in which Thomas Roberts had lived and to which, with such great eloquence, he had so frequently challenged others to live. And in this early winter of 1983, before Christmas, I later learned, Thomas Roberts ended his journey on earth and took up the place that God had prepared for him in heaven.

In my sojourn in the States I had spent time in fourteen cities in five states before my schedule called me back to Europe. That schedule meant I would break some new ground in the ministry during 1984, travelling for the first time into Holland, Denmark, Norway, Sweden and England. It also meant I would retravel much familiar terrain in France, Switzerland, Austria and Germany. By now I was holding follow-up meetings in Europe, just as I had in my early ministry in Texas and other states in the south-western and south-eastern United States. On such visits the ongoing work of the Holy Spirit in a community often can be seen, and rejoiced over. Also, seeds planted during previous visits can be watered and otherwise nurtured so that the eventual harvest will be bountiful. It is also a time for collecting testimonies of the way God's love has healed people, with enough time having passed to allow claimed healings to be put through medical checks.

31

'Do you love Jesus?'

My ministry in Europe brought a new challenge that February. Whereas over the fifteen previous months of ministry in the German-speaking lands I had been accompanied either by Fr Michael Marsch or by Gunter Oppermann and his team from Projektion-J, now I would travel alone. What was more, in each place in my schedule I had to train a team of people by myself to assist in the unfolding of my services. This, however, harked back to my experiences in the States and, indeed, also in other countries.

While I was ministering in Berlin, a question was impressed upon my heart, 'Do you love Jesus?' I quickly spoke it out. The question seemed so simple. But then I reflected, 'What are these people going to think?' Suddenly, I remembered that this, in effect, was the question that Jesus had asked Peter three times,[57] and my heart was comforted.

From that night on, for the next two years, this same question kept appearing in my heart, sometimes three or four times a service. And each time I perceived the question I would speak it out. Therefore, wherever I went, I was continually asking assemblies, 'Do you love Jesus?' What I also found out from people, either during or after the services, was that this call to a personal love relationship with Jesus, which I had imagined would be easy for any Christian to answer, for many turned out to be rather provocative and challenging.

Six months after this first question appeared, there came a second impression in the form of another question, 'Do you love his church?' And this question too I would speak out. And I would add, 'It's very difficult to love the head of the church, Jesus Christ, without loving his Body, too. You cannot divide the head from the Body, otherwise you do not truly have a love relationship with Jesus.'

---

[57] See John 21.15–19.

Near Kaufering, Germany, I was conducting a day-long seminar in a retreat house for about seventy charismatic Christians under the leadership of a Lutheran pastor. As it happened, a traditional Lutheran service, with communion, was held in this place on Saturday evenings. A young man who had come for the traditional service asked if he could stay for our charismatic praise and worship service, which was to follow. The pastor first told this young man 'no', because our service was designed for people who had been following the entire day's ministry. However, when the pastor saw how disappointed the young man looked, he relented and told him he could stay for the first half-hour of praise. So the young man stayed and also brought into our service a young woman friend. They sat against the back wall. As we began the service I noticed these two newcomers, but I did not yet know why they were there. After the half-hour of praise, the young woman got up and left, as the pastor had requested; the young man, however, did not budge. Three hours later, while our service continued, he had not moved.

Towards the end of prayer for individual needs the young man rose and came forward. I held out my hands to him, looked straight into his eyes and asked him, 'What do you want to pray for?' 'For my father and my mother,' he replied. As we began to pray a strong anointing of the Holy Spirit flooded over us and the young man fell back and rested in the Spirit.

'I don't think he knows Jesus,' the pastor whispered to me.

So when the young man stood up I said to him, 'Is Jesus Lord of your life? Jesus is the Way, the Truth and the Life, and no one can come to the Father except through him.[58] Jesus is here to meet you tonight; do you want to receive him?'

However, the young man said nothing. I continued: 'All we have to do is just kneel here and ask God to forgive your sins and ask Jesus to come into your heart.'

---

[58] See John 14.6.

He did kneel then and I knelt alongside him, and he broke down into tears, and then went into heavy sobbing.

After the service ended I went back and talked to the young man. I asked him if tonight had been the first time he had ever surrendered his life to Jesus, and he said, 'Yes.' Up to that point he had been studying the world's religions, comparing one with another.

I told the young man that Jesus had said to his apostles that it was expedient that the Master go away so that the Comforter, the Holy Spirit, would come upon them.[59] Did the young man want me also to pray for him that the Spirit would be poured out on him as he had been on the apostles at Pentecost?[60] And this too he agreed to. We prayed together again that he would have a 'personal Pentecost', and he received the Baptism of the Holy Spirit and began to speak in other tongues.

I did not ask the young man to tell me his name, but I did pray to the Lord, 'Please send him back for the next day's service.' When that service began, there was the young man, and he had brought the young woman along with him. She also came up for prayer and surrendered her life to Jesus and requested the prayer for the Baptism of the Holy Spirit, just as the young man had.

The Holy Spirit had pierced the young man's heart on Saturday, leading him to a conversion experience, and then moved him to persuade his friend to return to our meeting with him on Sunday. The wonders of his grace!

While I was ministering in France in mid-April I received word that my father had been taken to hospital with a bronchial condition. His doctor told me that I did not need to come home, that there was no major problem. Feeling temporarily reassured, I continued my schedule of ministry for another week, staying in daily contact with the hospital. Then, in my heart, I found a strong impulse to fly home to

---

[59] See John 16.7.   [60] See Acts 2.1–4.

my Dad in Florida. I notified the hospital of my coming and they said I would be able to take my father back to his home.

I left Germany on Good Friday and arrived in Orlando late the same day. I called the hospital and told them that I would be over shortly. A nurse informed me that the doctor had signed my father's discharge papers and that he would be ready for me to take him home. I rented a car and drove the two hours to the hospital.

When I got there it was about 10.0 pm. I found that my Dad's condition had changed drastically. When I entered his room he was unconscious. I was able to sit next to him for three hours, and I felt he knew I was there though he never awoke. Finally, while I kept my bedside vigil, Dad went home to the Lord. The tears I cried that night were more in joy than in sorrow, thankful as I was for the graces God had given my father and for his kindness in arranging for me to be present at his death.

On this same trip back to be with my father at his death, I found I was able to attend my son Robert's graduation from Midwest Bible Institute in Houston, which occurred shortly after my Dad's funeral. However, I unfortunately had to cancel plans for a later trip back to the States which would have let me attend Darin's graduation from high school. I was very proud of Darin though, as he had worked hard both at his studies and at football. He won local and state honours for football and was offered athletic scholarships by three universities; of the three, he accepted the one from Athens University in West Virginia.

Several days later, flying back across the Atlantic, and reflecting on the intensity of my walk with the Lord, I recollected the words impressed on my heart two years before in Israel—that the following two years of ministry abroad would be like being in school. Those two years were now ending and one thing had become clear: the United States was no longer home. My father's death, in fact, seemed to break a bond that had previously held me attached to the States.

Home! Where *was* home?

During the spring a number of people at services where I ministered testified to healings rendered by the Lord. In one case a word of knowledge came forth that a painful skin condition was being healed. A grandmother in the assembly received this word by faith in proxy for her eight-year-old grandson, who was at home and who had endured for years a condition of cracked and bleeding skin on both hands. The mother of this boy reported that his hands had become completely normal on the same evening, the skin soft and new as a baby's.

A second testimony told of a six-year-old boy who had been brought for prayer because of some eye problems. During this prayer he felt the power of the Holy Spirit enter his body. He was filled with an unusual joy, began to sing and dance and kept it up all the way home.

Several weeks later the boy's eye doctor, and two other doctors, found that certain of his ailments had disappeared. The eye doctor reported a healing from strabismus (being cross-eyed) and farsightedness. A doctor who regularly checked children at school verified the healing from 'psycho-motor disturbances' and also noted that the boy's extreme shyness was gone. His parents had been told that he would have to wait another year before starting school. Now the boy was able to commence his education immediately. A third doctor, a pediatrician, reported that the boy had been healed of a viral infection in the glands.

A few months before this healing this boy had given his life to the Lord. Following his experience of being healed, the boy, now even more full of faith, started to pray for the healings of other people. He also increased his reading of the Bible and manifested the gift of praying and singing in the Spirit (in tongues).

One year later this boy was again brought forward for prayer in one of my services. His parents said that the boy had had an accident in which his left elbow joint was broken into pieces. In a three-hour operation the pieces of bone were threaded back together on wires and the arm was put in a plaster cast. The incision, however, became badly infected and purulent, but the boy had to keep the cast on for three months. At that point the doctors X-rayed the joint, and the radiograph showed that one piece of bone was still missing. Plans were made to do a bone transplant. It was at this stage that we prayed for the boy during a service. We prayed that God would rebuild the bone and make it whole. And the next X-ray taken showed that this was in fact what had occurred. The bone transplant operation was cancelled.

32

Change of identity

I seemed to be at a watershed in my life. My father and mother now had both gone to their rest in God; my son Robert had just graduated from Midwest Bible School, and my son Darin was on the brink of graduating from high school. Both boys would embark upon university studies in the autumn; they were moving swiftly toward the beginning of adulthood. Clearly, the kinds of family responsibilities I had once tried to balance with my duties in ministry were diminishing, and I could feel God drawing me deeper and deeper into my calling as an instrument for reconciliation and unity.

What would come next? In the Lord, I have learned, the surprises go beyond even our own most creative scenarios for our lives. I had, in any case, a full schedule of ministry for late spring and summer in Europe, and I plunged back into it with a will. The miles rolled by as I criss-crossed central Europe by train—Zurich, Switzerland, to Pau and Bayonne in south-west France, north to Hochheim in Germany, back to Zurich, over to Stuttgart and, finally, to the Lion of Juda's major summer meeting in Ars, France.

The community had divided the meeting into two sessions of five days each, with a two-day break between the sessions. I did not experience anything particularly unusual in the first five-day session. However, at a Mass on the first day of the break, I once again found myself in tears.

Looking into my heart I could feel that God was completing my reconciliation with Mary and her role in the Catholic church, and, in a sense, my reconciliation with the Catholic church itself. My identity as a child had been Lutheran; my identity as an adult Christian had been with the inter-denominational Charismatic Renewal; and now, I could feel very strongly, my identity was to change.

The confirmation that I had waited upon for more than two years resonated in my heart. If ever God had spoken to me strongly during my seven years as a spirit-filled Christian, he was speaking to me now. He was inviting me to take my place in his Body as a member of the Catholic church.

For three days I underwent a heart-to-heart dialogue with God. I put many questions to the Lord, and I did not always get answers in the very specific forms that I might have desired. But the one thing I did receive was a peace that transcended all understanding.[61]

I remember asking the Lord, 'What about my son Robert? He has just finished an inter-denominational charismatic Bible school; how will he handle my step into the Catholic church?'

It was as if the Lord said to me in reply, 'Did you ask your children if you could give your life to me before you did it? Or did you live out that experience and then see what I would do with your children?'

Then I said, 'Lord, I have an entire evangelistic schedule for the autumn as an inter-denominational minister, including many meetings with Protestant, Pentecostal and inter-denominational groups in Norway, Sweden, and Denmark. What am I to tell them about this step?' I had no idea if every Protestant or Pentecostal door in Europe would be closed to me, nor how some Catholics would receive me—no idea what would happen to my life and my ministry.

The impression I received on my heart was this: 'This is

---

[61] See Philippians 4.7.

not *your* ministry; this is *my* ministry. And I've called you to walk in obedience; therefore be obedient unto me. Whatever happens it will not be your problem how to deal with it; it is up to me to deal with it.' A calm settled into my spirit, and I felt confident that the Lord would show me how to handle whatever situations might arise.

Another question I had for God was how to communicate the news to my brothers and sisters in other parts of the Body; how would they be able to comprehend why I was becoming a Catholic? I had an idea of the hardship my step would cause for many Christians who were active in the ecumenical realm, because many of them felt it was not right to change from one part of the Body to another.

Even at Ars, in a basically Catholic setting, I could not escape the pain of this sort of communication. Sharing my room with me during the Ars sessions was a young Lutheran student from Germany, Anita Schulz, who had been helping me with secretarial work for the last year. And she would be the first Protestant I would tell about my impending step. Also at this session was a Reformed pastor's wife, Ilma Furst, from Zurich, with her daughters. She and her husband Klaus and myself had worked very closely over the last three months with never a spoken word about a move like this on my part. I knew that I would have to find her and share the news.

'Lord . . . ! Lord . . !'

No, I did not then receive all the specific answers I would have liked, but, yes, I did receive an all-encompassing peace. At the end of my three days of dialogue with God I had never known such a total state of peace in all my life.

In an utter abandonment of my life and my ministry to my Lord, I had a profound inner sense that I was in God's perfect will for me at that moment.

One participant in the sessions of teaching and praise was Mgr Jean Chabbèrt, the bishop that Ephraim and I had spoken about as we strolled through a vineyard at Pont Saint Esprit two years earlier. Mgr Chabbèrt had indeed returned to France from Morocco and had been assigned to shepherd the diocese of Perpignan on France's western Mediterranean coast. I asked Ephraim if he would schedule an appointment for me with this bishop that I might tell him that I felt God was calling me to enter the Catholic church.

Mgr Chabbèrt and I went over a number of key doctrinal understandings together. He also agreed to oversee my ministry, then he charged me to develop that ministry in close relationship with the Lion of Juda. The community was to be my new spiritual family.

My baptism was acknowledged as fully valid. The Catholic church usually accepts baptism as a sacrament[62] in whatever Christian tradition that baptism was administered. I had never, however, been confirmed as a Lutheran, and so Mgr. Chabbèrt decided it would be good if I was confirmed immediately and my confirmation was woven into the Ars celebration. As a preparation for that, I received the Sacrament of Reconciliation.

On the day of my confirmation I rose at 7.0 am. I wanted to go and spend a time in prayer. I was on my way from the building where I was lodged to a little chapel, where the Holy Sacrament was exposed, when I encountered Ilma Furst walking up the road. She asked me if I was 'going through' with the step. I told her I was. We started to walk

---

[62] A 'Sacrament' in Catholic understanding is an outward sign signifying the transmission of grace. The Catholic church recognises seven sacraments: Baptism, Reconciliation (Confession), Eucharist (Communion), Confirmation, Marriage, Ordination, and the Sacrament of the Sick (Extreme Unction). As Alan Schreck, an associate professor of theology at the Franciscan University of Steubenville, Ohio, explains, 'Sacraments are simply channels through which the grace of God, flowing from the cross of Jesus, comes to us. They are (however) not the only channels of God's grace through Jesus, but they are reliable channels that never run dry ... We must participate in the sacraments not merely externally, but with real faith and expectancy that God himself is present there and wishes to act in our lives through them.' See A. Schreck, *Catholic and Christian*, Servant Books, Ann Arbor, Michigan, pp119–120.

together and then sat down on a low stone wall and fell into each other's arms, weeping. It felt like all the bitter hurts caused by the divisions and centuries of strife in the Body of Christ were slashing through our hearts. Feeling the pain that Ilma was suffering as I moved from the Protestant side to the Catholic side of the Body was almost too much for me to bear.

During the closing Mass at Ars on August 2, 1984, Mgr Chabbèrt received me into the Catholic church and administered to me the sacrament of confirmation. In doing so he anointed my forehead with the oil of chrism[63] as he imprinted the sign of the cross there with his thumb.

It was another important 'way station' in my journey with the Lord toward the realisation of his will for my life and my ministry. It was a way station I approached with great joy, even though I had already experienced some of my friends' pain and perceived that there would be more painful encounters ahead.

Opening the Mass Mgr Jean Chabbèrt said to the five thousand assembled in the crypt: 'Brothers and sisters, the Lord is present among us as he was on Easter evening when he presented himself to his apostles. And to us, also gathered, he says, "Peace be with you. Look at the wounds in my hands, in my feet; look at the wound in my side. Do not stop looking at me, do not stop contemplating me, do not stop admiring me. It is really me, Jesus, risen, living, Lord and Christ, Son of God."

'This is our faith: Jesus is risen.

'And in the same way in which he breathed his Spirit onto his apostles on Easter evening, he is also going to renew us today by the sacrament of confirmation that our sister Kim is going to receive and that we have received, in which all the action of the Spirit has its source, even if this action manifests itself before the sacrament has been received. But it is the sacrament which gives deep roots.

---

[63] Special oil blessed by a bishop on Holy Thursday which is used to signify a 'fullness of grace'.

'That is why it is a joy for us to hear today the testimony of our sister, who is going to tell us how the Spirit of the Lord guided her all along her life so that today she may surrender herself totally to the will of the Lord for her in our church.'

As I arose my heart was inflamed in God's love and I perceived a strong anointing of the Holy Spirit when I started to speak: 'Today ends a journey that began and was ordained even before my birth.

'I met Jesus as a child; however, in my early teenage years I became very rebellious. I began to go my own way. This rebellion lasted for over twenty years. I was like the Prodigal Son.

'But in the twelfth year of those twenty years something began to stir in my heart again. I knew something was missing in my life, but I did not know exactly what. I believed in God. I felt I had a mission to fulfil but I did not know for whom. I continued walking and seeking for eight more years.

'Finally, I found my way home. I tried many paths trying to find God during those eight years. They were paths that led to dead-end roads. Then one night I was invited to go to an inter-confessional charismatic prayer group and it was on this night that I found my way home. Through Jesus I was reconciled with the Father.

'I said, "Lord, here is my life; do whatever you want with it." I received the Baptism of the Holy Spirit that night. I also received a prophetic word confirming what I had held in my heart for eight years—that there was a mission that I had to fulfil.

'Things began to happen very fast. This was in 1978. Within three weeks the Lord had shown me that he wanted me to move from Florida to Texas. I became part of a large inter-confessional community there. Then the Lord moved me to a smaller community and it was there that the call to full-time service came. That community shared their love with me and blessed me to send me forth on the mission that God had given me.

'The Lord showed me that my ministry would begin in a region and then would extend throughout the United States and then become international. Just as he had shown it to me, it took place . . .' and I went on to outline the events described in these pages.

I concluded: 'I saw God's hand as he continued to lead me into different parts of his Body, calling and bringing forth that reconciliation of his Body. But it was here, on Saturday, during Mass, as I looked at the icon of Mary and Jesus, that the same tears came. There was no longer any question of where home was. Today, I enter that home. Amen.'

It would be months before my head caught up with my heart, however. Psychologically, I did not then feel prepared for God's timing of my entrance into the Catholic church. I had waited two years for the Lord to confirm that this was my place in the Body and when after the first year no confirmation had come, I had just put the idea to the side. I have learned only too well in my journey with the Lord, however, that when his time for a new step arrives, things can happen quickly. He had called me to obedience and I had submitted my whole self to that call, to follow him no matter where he led. And my step into the Catholic church that day took the form of an act of love, lived out in obedience to my Lord.

Thus far there had been three times when I experienced being drawn to a point of total surrender in my walk with the Lord. As I surrendered and accepted what I perceived was his will for me in each instance, something inside of me died—and more of his life flooded my being. My first 'yes' came in 1980 in response to His inviting me to leave the business world and enter evangelistic service. That call involved giving up my secular financial security and deciding to trust God as my provider of money and other material resources. The second 'yes' occurred in 1982 when the Lord asked me to give up my house outside Dallas and take off for what presumably would be a new life in Europe—but with no clear idea of where I would live. This second call meant forsaking my American cultural context; even more importantly, it meant putting an ocean between me and my sons. Now there had come this third 'yes', this relocation of my spiritual life from the inter-denominational charismatic dimension into the heart of the Catholic church.

As in the first two calls to abandonment, I lived out this third call in a spirit of total dependence upon God. I did not yet really know how to walk in my ministry as a 'Catholic': God would have to teach me. I did not know what would happen to my ministry; but that too was in God's hands, not mine. All I had to do was walk along the path he had prepared for me, staying in his light, not moving either too slowly or too fast, just one day at a time. The way would be shown.

That evening, after the gathering at Ars finished, the participants having trickled back to cars and driven off, some 250 members of the Lion of Juda lingered on the grounds to help with the clearing up. There then followed a special session for the community, at which I was asked to minister. The Lord bestowed on the assembly a strong prophetic anointing, which was quite unusual. As each house of the community was cited aloud and members of that house invited to come forward for prayer, I received specific prophecies for that house. Even more, there were prophetic words for virtually every member. The sense of the Lord's blessing upon us all was tremendous.

My schedule for ministry following my conversion into the Catholic faith was full and included many meetings with Protestant brothers and sisters—few of whom yet knew that I had become a Catholic. My first stop was in the Biarritz-Bayonne-Anglet area in south-west France, ministering in the Tent of Unity, an inspiration of Thomas Roberts. The evangelisation campaign there had been among the last events he had been able to plan before his death.

Everyone connected with the Tent, of course, had been expecting me to appear as a Protestant. When I told my brothers and sisters gathered for this ministry that I had just been confirmed as a Catholic, there was great surprise and, on the part of some Protestants, shock. The Lord, however, especially in the generous outpouring of his Holy Spirit, overcame our differences and brought us into a period of acceptance and harmony through love. Especially instrumental in this process were Jean-Daniel Fischer, a French Reformed pastor, and his wife, Marie-Louise.

Out of my entire autumn schedule only two meetings were cancelled, one by a Pentecostal group, the other—and here the Lord's sense of humour was evident—by a Catholic group who had not yet heard of my step and thought I was 'too Protestant'. As I walked among the parts of the Lord's body, one day among Catholics, another day among Protestants and so forth, I truly felt the favour of God's grace.

My concern about the reaction of my son Robert to my conversion also had a humorous outcome. When I returned to the States for Christmas 1984 he began to tell me about a girl he had begun dating. Yes, she was Christian, but she was also Catholic. It was this girl, Jennifer Koos, that Robert was to marry eighteen months later.

Those in my own country from other parts of Christ's Body with whom I had worked closely in the past had, I found, an incredible openness to receive me in Jesus just where I was. Even though they often could not understand why I had changed from Protestant to Catholic, they accepted me and loved me. I couldn't find the words to tell them how much this agape love meant to me.

Moreover, when I saw the pastor from whose church I had been sent forth, Marvin Crow, and described to him my confirmation as a Catholic in Ars, our time together was *very* blessed. Not one particle of our oneness in Christ was broken. He accepted me completely and supported me in the step I had taken.

33

New meanings

Now I took stock: I was Catholic; what was more, the ministry was attached to a French Catholic charismatic community, the Lion of Juda, which now had thirteen houses in France and others in Morocco, Zaïre, Italy and

Israel. Yet, just two months before, I had accepted the offer of a guest room that I might use in central Germany. What was the purpose of my having that room? Had I misunderstood God when I agreed to accept it? Should I give up that room and ask for a room in one of the Lion of Juda houses in France? After all, my bishop was also in France.

In addition I found that the question of where my home was had not been completely resolved after all. Geographically, was I supposed to base my ministry in France, where the Lion of Juda had so many houses? The logical answer might have been 'yes'. But Germany was the land of my ancestry. I had by now begun to speak basic conversational German, and if anyone had asked me which European country I identified with most, I would quickly have named Germany.

Where do you want me to live, Lord? I would ask. However, I did not receive any immediate answer, just an inner silence. I decided to make no changes and just keep the room in Germany pending some clear direction from God. In my dreams I would often toss the question over: Where was my geographical and cultural home? Which land should I live in? Not even in my dreams, however, did I find any answer.

At the end of August I was to launch out on my first Scandinavian tour: forty days that would span Norway, Sweden and Denmark. In the midst of this period I would have to fly to Zurich for a five-day meeting at the eighth European Ecumenical Charismatic Leaders' Conference, where I would also minister.

The first part of the tour, in Norway, went well, and I was just getting under way with my schedule in Sweden when I received an urgent phone call from my son Darin. What had appeared to be working out so well for him just a few weeks before as he arrived at Athens University in West Virginia had suddenly turned into a shambles. He injured a knee in football practice at the university and was told that he would not be able to play that year. What's more, his scholarship was now jeopardised. Next, the two-year relationship Darin had had with a girlfriend broke up. On the phone now Darin asked me if he could leave and come and spend time with me in Europe. I arranged for him to fly to Frankfurt immediately and stay with the young people from Projektion-J until I returned there from Scandinavia.

While in Stockholm I was received into the home of Siv and Robert Pellen, who had organised my meetings in that city. This couple had been active in the European Ecumenical Charismatic Leaders' conferences. As publishers of a magazine serving the Charismatic Renewal in Sweden, they had files of material on the conference since its inception. Looking through their files familiarised me with the history of the conference.

I also read an account of the 1977 Kansas City Conference on Charismatic Renewal in the Christian Churches. The American conference brought together fifty thousand people from more than a dozen denominations for four days to join in proclaiming the theme, 'Jesus is Lord'. I could see that the European Strasbourg Congress in 1982 was very much like this gathering.

Continuing in my reading of the Kansas City accounts, I came upon prophetic words given through Ralph Martin:

Mourn and weep, for the body of my Son is broken.

Mourn and weep, for the body of my Son is broken.

Come before me with broken hearts and contrite spirits, for the body of my Son is broken.

Come before me with sackcloth and ashes, come before me with tears and mourning, for the body of my Son is broken.

As my eyes moved down the page, I felt the words electrifying my spirit and causing me to break into heavy sobbing, almost uncontrollable sobbing. I felt I was somehow entering into the pain of the Father looking down on his Son's shattered body on earth.

It was quite a long time before I could regain enough composure to read on:

I would have made you one new man, but the body of my Son is broken.

I would have made you a light on a mountaintop, a city glorious and splendrous that all the world would have seen, but the body of my Son is broken.

The light is dim. My people are scattered. The body of my Son is broken.

Turn from the sins of your fathers. Walk in the ways of my Son. Return to the plan of your Father, return to the purpose of your God.

The body of my Son is broken . . .

My walk with the Lord, weaving in and out of so many different denominations, even without my knowing it, had been caught up with a response to that anguishing prophecy heard in Kansas City. I felt overcome, and humbled, to see how God had been using the ministry as an instrument to help bring together the broken pieces of Jesus' body.

I also found it remarkable to realise that at the time the prophecy had been given I was thirty-three years old and still far from the Lord. Now my whole life was a response to that prophecy. How great is our God's mercy, how strange are his ways.

On September 18 I flew from Stockholm to Zurich for the eighth European Ecumenical Charismatic Leaders' Conference. This gathering, as I had gleaned from the Pellens' files, had a short but illustrious history. It had helped to forge ecumenical relationships among some of the major figures in the charismatic movement in England and on the Continent.

In the early stages of the Renewal, David du Plessis visited charismatic groups in Europe and invited a number of leaders to come together for certain specific purposes. These were: to share what the Lord was doing all around Europe; to listen to the Lord in what he was saying, and to deepen relationships between the various denominations in the renewal. It was during the fifth of these meetings, in Malines, Belgium, in 1976, that Thomas Roberts submitted his vision for the large pan-European charismatic conference held in Strasbourg in 1982.

The place where the present meeting was to be held, in Nidelbach/Ruschlikon near Zurich, is one of the oldest centres of Christian ecumenism in the world. I will never forget the precious spirit of generosity and love with which Klaus Furst, the Reformed church pastor from Zurich, introduced me to the conference. Confessing he himself did not fully understand my step into the Catholic church, he called for all to welcome me in my new Catholic identity, no less a sister in the Lord than before.

The worship area in this ecumenical centre was architecturally designed to represent the divisions in the Body and to provide avenues for reconciliation. Singing 'Father, make us one!'[64] we moved in two processions from the chapels into the Room of the Brethren.

In this room is a basin for footwashing into which new water continually drips.[65] A Catholic priest began by asking to wash the feet of a brother from a Pentecostal church and, in doing so, asked him to forgive him and the Catholic church for the things Catholics had said against the Pentecostal church and for the division between their churches. The priest also asked that God heal him for wounds he had received from what Pentecostals had said against Catholics. Then a Lutheran pastor washed the feet of a Baptist pastor. Others followed and began to wash one another's feet as the Holy Spirit led them to ask for forgiveness and healing.

After the brothers and sisters of the diverse churches had washed each other's feet, one of the leaders placed a lighted Jewish menorah (candelabra) in the basin of water as a symbol that the Jewish people were part of this time of reconciliation.

Leaving the Room of the Brethren through the two side chapels we sang the chorus, 'We are one in the Spirit, we are one in the Lord . . .'

God's healing love was liberated in our hearts that day through our mutual humbling of ourselves and our forthright begging of forgiveness from one another. A healing of the wounds of division took place in our hearts, even if only a partial one; still more healing, we recognised, needed to

---

[64] See John 17.20–23.   [65] See John 13.1–17.

occur in us, a small number of Christians, for us to become truly one again. How much healing was still needed in the Body of Christ worldwide!

After the conference closed, the participants led an open charismatic service at the large Zurich Reformed Church of Fraumunster. My son Darin came by train from Frankfurt to join me for this service and to spend some time together. He came straight to the church after his arrival. I was engaged in pre-meeting preparations. Still tired from jet lag from his trip from the States, he went to the back of the church, lay down on a pew, and fell asleep. Forty minutes later he opened his eyes, looked around and was astonished to see that the church had filled up. Now there were 1,200 people all around him. Darin had attended only one of my services previously, in 1980, and that day there had been forty people present.

34

Forgiving—again

During the same autumn the Lord allowed some old wounds buried deep in my spirit to surface. Simultaneously, I underwent suffering from some new hurts. What triggered a seeming avalanche of inner pain was Darin's situation, and the financial burdens that had come with it.

It had now been fifteen years since I had been left alone as a mother to raise my two boys. For a long while I deluded myself that I had forgiven my husband for leaving me with the responsibility for the children. But I discovered that deep inside me a great anger had been smouldering over my having had to shoulder almost all the expenses of child rearing. The father's child support contributions had been sporadic at best.

I also found an anger inside me toward both of my sons for the various financial crises in which they had become involved. These crises had frequently meant that 'Mom' was the solution. Besides this, I was angry with other people whom I thought had been unfair to me financially in the course of my ministry.

I recognised a pattern: in each case I felt I had been misused; in each case the unfair treatment had caused me many serious problems.

Over the next month it seemed I was pushed to my absolute limits. As always in such an extreme state, I began to do what I had so frequently done before: to cry out, 'Lord, help!' I realised that the only answer was forgiveness. Even though I had forgiven before, I did not find it any easier this time to go through the steps.

On a train trundling across Austria in mid-November I found myself feeling very angry and depressed. I said inwardly, 'Lord, I just need your help!'

God was faithful. He was ready to help me right then. But I didn't want to hear what he had to say. I had an inner sense that I should look into the Gospel of Luke. As I did so, God used his Word to speak to me: 'But I say this to you who are listening: Love your enemies, do good to those who hate you, bless those who curse you and pray for those who treat you badly. To the man who slaps you on one cheek, present the other cheek as well; to the man who takes your cloak from you, do not refuse your tunic. Give to everyone who asks you, and do not ask for your property back from the man who robs you' (Luke 6.27–30).

I thought to myself, 'I know those scriptures; I know them well.' And I felt that I had given everything I had to give. How, I asked myself, could I give any more?

I began to say to God, 'It's not fair! It's not fair!'

I was not expecting an answer; I was just caught up in my own self-pity. However, I got an answer anyway. The words that came into my heart at that moment were, 'Do you think it was fair for Jesus? Was it fair that he took your sins upon him, so that you might be set free? Was it fair that he paid your debt, *a debt he did not owe*?'

Of course I already knew the answers to these questions. And I also received an understanding that my definition of what was 'fair' was not the same as God's. As long as I live upon this earth I will encounter situations that I will feel are unfair. Did my Lord not invite me, however, to deny myself, take up my cross and follow him? Then I knew that some 'unfair' burden could never again cause the wounds that I had suffered before. But I was just beginning to understand more deeply about forgiveness, how absolute real forgiveness had to be—not depending upon what the offending person did. I started to see that we are called to forgive others as completely as Christ forgives us.[66] To forgive absolutely, not conditionally.

That's when I took out a pad and pencil and began to make a list of the wounds I had in my heart and of the people with whom I was angry.

First, I was angry with God. In truth, though, I was angry with myself. I was hurt by and angry with the children's father . . . with my children . . . and with people who, I felt, had misused me in connection with ministry.

If we find a wound or an anger in our heart, that is almost always a sign that we have not gone through the process of forgiving someone else completely.

With my list finished it was time to start the process of forgiving. I first asked God to forgive me for my anger toward him. As I said, I really wasn't angry with God; I just wanted someone else to blame besides myself.

Then I went down my list, and one after another, went through with forgiving each.

I had some interesting insights as I tried to forgive my children. For one thing I came to the realisation that I had rarely forgiven them for anything in their lives. For another thing I saw that I had always been someone who cherished having a very positive attitude toward life. Thus, whenever I received wounds from the children, instead of forgiving them and letting the wounds be healed, I would bury the wounds deep within me. Furthermore, I would justify this by saying to myself, 'It's only their age. They'll grow out of it. It would

---

[66] See Mark 11.25, Luke 17.4, Ephesians 4.32 and Colossians 3.13.

be different if they had a father here.' But I never forgave; I always justified. This meant that the wounds were always within me and could be brought to the surface suddenly.

In trying to forgive the children's father I really began to understand what God was saying. Was I willing to release him forever from his financial responsibilities, past and present, for the children? Was I willing, that is, to practise absolute forgiveness? The answer was no. I *thought* I wanted to forgive, but true forgiveness would have meant being willing to accept and come to terms with what had happened to me and to release him from any responsibility for what he had done to us. I did not want to release him from his obligations.

It was only some time after I worked my way through forgiving the children's father that I came upon material comparing steps in forgiveness to steps in dying.[67] In research on 'death and dying' some psychologists have identified the following five steps: 1. Denial, 2. Anger, 3. Bargaining, 4. Depression, and 5. Acceptance. I believe that in my case I touched on each of the five, although not every one necessarily passes through all five of the steps before accepting 'death' or giving total forgiveness.

First, for such a long time I had denied that there even were any wounds in my heart. I had taken the attitude, 'They're my children and I'll provide for them.'

Second, the anger in me was so intense and the bitterness so deep that these two emotions were almost destroying my heart.

Third, I reached the point where I was willing to forgive, but only conditionally. 'I'll forgive him if he begins to do something now about his responsibilities, if he takes more time with the boys, if he pays me what he owes.' Or, 'At least I'd like him to say he's sorry for the wrong he has done.' What I wanted to do was to bargain my way to forgiveness.

---

[67] These 'steps' are discussed more fully in Dennis and Matthew Linn's book, *Healing Life's Hurts: Healing Memories through the Stages of Forgiveness*, Paulist Press, New York.

But that is not the kind of forgiveness that God asks of us. It took me a long time, however, to get past this point.

Fourth, I started to find myself becoming depressed. My anger was no longer turned outward, but rather inward against myself. I was angry at myself for allowing the children's father to misuse me, angry that I had not done something about it before. My heart felt heavy and sad; if I could have drawn a picture of it, I would have coloured it dark grey . . .

Fifth, was I ready to accept that I had been hurt, accept the consequences of those hurts and still practise God's kind of forgiveness?

No, I wasn't. It would take me another four months before I reached the point of saying yes.

When I finally reached that point I decided to write the children's father a letter. In the letter I told him that I forgave him for what I perceived as all his past mistakes and asked him to forgive me for the wounds I might have caused him. I also said that I released him from all the unpaid child support he owed me.

My writing that letter was in effect like tearing up a debtor's notes so that they could never be used against him again.[68] And this is what God calls us to do each time we try to forgive someone. 'Forgive us our debts as we forgive our debtors' is what we so often pray, and so seldom achieve. But God wants us to change, really change, and become true channels of his forgiveness to one another.

Each time I reached the point of totally forgiving people who had hurt me, I experienced God's love filling the wounds inside of me and closing them up. I also experienced feelings of being set free from pain and resentment that I had harboured.

Something else happened when I became willing to forgive the children's father. My unforgiveness somehow had helped cripple their relationships with each other, both father and sons. This was so despite the fact that I had

---

[68] See Matthew 18.21–35.

always tried to promote good relationships between them. And now my act of forgiveness was having a positive effect —it was a catalyst for a healing of their own hurt relationships.

One classic example dealt with gifts for Christmas, birthdays or other special occasions. For a long time there was a standing joke in the family: Dad's gifts to the boys were always 'in the mail' but they never arrived. After I sent my letter of forgiveness, there was a drastic change. The gifts began to arrive. For the first time in his life my son Darin went out and bought his Dad a Father's Day card and took it over to his house. And father and son ended up embracing each other in tears.

Are we willing to pay the price to forgive as God forgives? That is a question each of us must ask ourselves. Yes, the price is high, especially in the swallowing of hurt pride. Remember, however, that the Lord does not ask us to forgive in our own strength, but rather through the power of the Holy Spirit that dwells within us.

My son Darin was visiting me in Europe that autumn. He had come with many wounds in his heart on the heels of substantial setbacks in his school and personal life. As a mother I recognised his hurts, anger and bitterness and tried to talk to him and help him understand God's principles of forgiveness. It was like talking to a wall. Nothing penetrated.

As he travelled with me in the ministry, Darin often heard me teach on the topic of forgiveness. One day he came to me after a meeting and said, 'Mom, that wasn't too bad. I even began to feel something inside of me.' I smiled at him and thought, 'The Holy Spirit is at work.'

Then, during a time of individual prayer at a meeting I was conducting, I looked up and found that the next person waiting to be prayed with was my son. He asked me to pray for him that God might help him to forgive others and also heal his heart. What a joy for a mother who was also a minister of the gospel to see the Holy Spirit so clearly at work in her child.

That year, 1984, forgiveness took on a new reality in my

life and in my ministry. The numerous painful experiences I had undergone had called me to greater depths of forgiveness and reconciliation. In passing through those experiences in a spirit of abandonment to God I felt the healing power of forgiveness close old wounds in my heart. And I was ready to move on.

For Christmas Darin and I flew back to the States to join Robert for our annual holiday as a family. Darin had by then decided he wanted to work for a while and then return to college the following autumn. Robert was now enrolled in Ashland College in Ohio, where he was concentrating on studies in communications.

With things looking positive for my sons, I returned to Europe, where a heavy schedule of ministry awaited me. Soon after my departure, Darin found a job in Orlando and also found a room-mate with whom to share an apartment.

Once again, however, catastrophe struck. As Darin was driving along an expressway in Orlando, something hit the motor casing of the car and the motor was badly damaged. My son was told he would need to replace the motor completely. The cost: a thousand dollars, which neither Darin nor I had available.

I was able, however, to secure a loan for Darin with which he could pay for the car repairs. Since his new room-mate was a master mechanic, Darin decided to entrust him with the work, and gave him money to purchase the parts.

While the room-mate was lifting out the old, damaged motor and getting into the repair job, however, Darin went away for a weekend. Upon his return, he could not believe the situation that he saw: his car was in pieces, most of his belongings had been stolen from the apartment, and the room-mate was gone, taking with him the money Darin had given him for parts. Worse, the delinquent room-mate had not turned in the rent money Darin had left for him to pass to the landlord, and had run up close to four hundred dollars in telephone calls, leaving Darin responsible for the bill. The landlord came over and bluntly notified him that he had three days to move out.

WHERE IS HOME?

I was in Paris when I received a phone call from my son, who talked to me in sobs as he sat on the kitchen floor of a nearly empty apartment. When is it ever going to stop? I asked myself as I listened to my second son's latest plight. Ever since I had made my final commitment to seek the Lord, I had faced crisis after crisis. Many of the crises had occurred in my children's lives, some in my own. Either way I was deeply affected by each of them.

The only way I survived these crises was by clinging to God's promises to us in his Word. And in the midst of the current crisis, I resorted to them again, promises such as: 'And we know that in all things God works for the good of those who love him, who have been called according to his purposes' (Romans 8.28); 'Cast all your anxiety on him, because he cares for you' (1 Peter 5.7); 'Be joyful always; pray continually; give thanks in all circumstances, for this is God's will for you in Christ Jesus' (1 Thessalonians 5.16–18).

Gradually, Darin's situation improved. He was able to find an honest room-mate with whom to share another apartment, a place that, this time, was close enough to his job so that he could walk to work. Over the course of four months he saved up enough money to have his car repaired. Just two days after he had got it back, however, a large truck smashed into its rear end in a supermarket parking lot and fled from the scene. My son was left with his car undriveable again, and the exasperation of having to earn and save up more money for repairs. Happily, Darin reacted much more calmly to the second situation, and I was able to praise the Lord that both of us dealt with the new setback without letting ourselves become burdened with frustration. More stable and settled, Darin returned to college that autumn.

35

What next, Lord?

In the spring of 1985, acting upon a strong impulse I had first felt four months before, I drew aside for a time of stillness, prayer and reflection. I also felt God calling me to a long fast. I set aside forty days beginning on Palm Sunday to undertake this retreat in a small convent in the Austrian mountains near Schruns. I hoped that during this time God would give me an understanding of what lay ahead in my ministry —and where home was.

I entered into this retreat exhausted and sick with a cold. Each day I had a long period of prayer and reflection. I attended daily Mass and had one-hour talks each day about my spiritual life with the Mother Superior, Sister Marguerita.

I waited for strong experiences with the Lord, for thunder and lightning, crystal-clear revelations of what he had ahead for me. Instead, I received virtually nothing at all. It seemed, in fact, rather as if I had entered another time of uncertainty. All I perceived, vaguely, was an idea of forming an advisory council for my ministry in the German-speaking countries. I also received something I had not actually been looking for but which was quite a blessing: an inner healing from fears that had begun to inhibit my openness to the Holy Spirit's leadings during services. This healing came about while I was drawn to reread the life story of St Catherine of Siena. What spoke strongly to my heart this time, were these points: that St Catherine had lived a very radical Christianity, that she had undergone a lot of sharp criticism of her ministry but that she had clung to a fervent obedience to her superiors. When the forty days ended and I was on my way out of the convent, however, had you asked me what the next step in my life would be, I would have been totally unable to tell you.

That was not to say at all that the forty-day retreat had

been futile for finding direction; it had not. For one thing I explored the idea of an advisory council. First, I checked with Mgr Chabbèrt, my bishop, and received his approval. I had upon my heart four individuals, all Jesuit priests, and I made an appointment with one, Professor Norbert Baumert, SJ, who taught New Testament theology at St Georgen University in Frankfurt. He agreed to serve on such a council and to contact the other Jesuits. Our first meeting was held a month later. The council provided me with an informal forum to discuss theological issues and questions about any area of my ministry in relationship to the German-speaking countries.

As to the question of what the next step in my life would be, I had to recognise that God's ways are not our ways, and, very frequently, his timing is not our timing. Nothing I could have done could have 'forced' God to reveal his plans for me before he was ready. Even the forty days of stillness and prayer could not guarantee an immediate response. God would respond to my questions—but in his time.

That time arrived three months after my retreat, on August 10, while I was ministering in Germany. While I was praying and preparing for my next morning's service I felt a question impressed on my spirit. The question was, 'What day is this?'

'That's a funny question,' I thought. 'Well, it's August 10 today.'

Then came another question, 'When was the first day of your ministry?'

The date has always been fixed firmly in my mind: it was August 9, 1980. Five years had gone by. Then the impression continued, 'The first phase of your ministry is now behind you.'

Suddenly, I knew a second five-year phase was going to begin. I perceived that it was to be a phase when I would continue to live and minister in Europe, a phase in which the Lord would take me into a deeper understanding of his church, a time of maturing in my knowledge of him and of his Body: a time of a different anointing on the ministry. And after this next five-year phase in Europe, I could also perceive, God would push back the frontiers and send the ministry beyond Europe to other continents. New missions were coming; but I did not yet know what they were.

Shortly after that, it was time for me to return to Ars. It would be my first anniversary of becoming a Catholic. Two German friends came with me this time, Anita Schulz and Maria Wissen. Anita was still helping me with secretarial work. Maria, who was Catholic, directed counselling services for women in the diocese of Munich; she had lately been feeling that the Lord wanted her to participate in the founding of a charismatic community in Germany. Maria had come to Ars to learn about the community style of the Lion of Juda; in fact, at her request, I had also arranged for her to visit Lion of Juda houses at Nay and Cordes in France.

While I was at Ars, however, in the midst of the Lion of Juda's major annual celebration of God's love for all people, a part of an understanding that I had been waiting for came to me—during a Mass on August 23; only it was *not* something I was very open to receive.

I received a strong impression on my heart telling me that I was being called to take responsibility for the founding of a community in the German-speaking countries. The impression also showed me that God would bless abundantly, as he had in France. However, I had no desire at all to do what it appeared God was asking me to do.

These impressions were almost more than I could deal with. I felt that I had gone through so much in the last five years that I needed more time just to assimilate what had happened to me. I had by then ministered across many denominational lines in eighteen countries and many different cultures. I had been coming into contact with fifty thousand people a year. And everything had been intensified because of my step into the Catholic church and my need then to account for this step in so many Protestant and Pentecostal circles, which had taken substantial reservoirs of energy. What I needed more than anything else, I felt, was a rest.

Nonetheless, I decided to talk to Ephraim to see if the

community could be open to developing into the German-speaking countries. I learned that the Lion of Juda leaders were not particularly interested in this idea. Despite their lack of immediate interest, I remained open in my heart, waiting to see the results of Maria Wissen's visits to the two Lion of Juda houses. Anita, Maria and I even went so far as to celebrate, by faith, the founding of a charismatic community in Germany. We did this by going to the chapel to pray together and then by sharing a meal in our room at Ars and calling it the first meal of the German community.

Things grew more complex however when Maria returned to Germany in early September after she had visited the Lion of Juda houses in France. 'No,' she told me by telephone, 'the German community is not supposed to be a house of the Lion of Juda.' Overwhelmed by the whole project, I put the idea aside, hoping that maybe the Lord would tap someone else for this task. I tried to get my mind focused on other things.

What I have learned, though, is that when God wants to direct you in a certain path, he will gently reinforce his impressions on your heart and persist—as long as your heart stays open and pliable—until he draws you into an understanding of how you should proceed.

I plunged into my autumn evangelistic schedule as the best means of getting away from these unsettling impressions. However, on the evening of September 11 in Karlsruhe, Germany, I experienced what I believe was a change in my ministry. In that evening's meeting, sponsored by a Catholic prayer group and held in a Catholic parish with over two hundred present, I felt an extraordinary awareness of God's love and a very powerful anointing of the Holy Spirit. In meetings such as this over the previous five years, my ministry had always been accompanied by people's resting in the Spirit as they were prayed for individually. That night no resting in the Spirit occurred. What was more, from that night forward, resting in the Spirit did not take place unless I was sharing in someone else's ministry where this experience usually occurred.

At Karlsruhe, too, there came another interesting change.

I felt that the Lord was asking that, instead of our having just a single team of three praying for individuals, there be three or even more teams of two. It also felt as if the Lord was saying that he would bless each team with his anointing for that service through a blessing of the teams by the pastor or priest who was presiding.

36

'This will be our chapel'

Next came what I would call my second major visitation from the Lord. It was an experience very similar to what I had had in 1980 when the Lord had called me into evangelistic service.

Again I was in my room in the evening, this time in personal conversation with Anita. It was about 10.0 pm on a Friday. She and I were in the midst of a discussion about how, from time to time, I felt such a dying away inside myself, that Kim Kollins didn't even exist anymore, that my whole being just felt in abandonment to God, to fulfil whatever plans he had made for me.[69] Suddenly God's glory filled the room. The lighting seemed to change to reflect the new radiance. Anita experienced this change with me.

I then asked if she would please let me have this time alone with the Lord. As she left the room I lit a candle at my prayer altar. I felt God saying, 'I want to make a new covenant with you. It will not be easy; the cost will be high.' With these words came an overwhelming manifestation of God's love, something almost palpable in the air that permeated the whole room. It made me feel totally secure, and at peace, like being held in the arms of the Father.

It also felt as if God were saying, 'You can say yes or no.' Without any other words I perceived that if I said no, the

---

[69] See John 12.24–25.

Father would not be angry with me, that I had a total liberty to choose. The question hung in the air for forty minutes while God's radiance continued to be manifested.

Finally, I said a new 'yes' to my Father for whatever he was calling upon me to do. There was as yet no indication or no thought of just what this might be. I said yes in a completely blind dimension, simply telling the Father that I would be open to whatever he had prepared for me.

The next day I tried in my heart and in my thoughts to recapture the experience, because it had been so powerful, beautiful and blessed. Such experiences, however, are impossible to bring back. I had to content myself with a faint impression of what I had lived with the Lord.

As I fell asleep that night, Saturday, September 14, however, I found myself having a dream with spiritual meaning, the first such dream I had ever had. What stayed with me after I woke up was just the very last scene of that dream: I was showing two of the sisters from the Lion of Juda through a house and as I opened a door to a large room I said to them, 'This will be our chapel.'

I awoke with a clear understanding of the words that had been placed in my heart three weeks earlier, that I must be willing to take responsibility for founding communities in the German-speaking countries. I also felt that God was definitely confirming the notion that the houses were to be of the Lion of Juda. I found myself, just after waking, with a faith and an anointing stronger than anything I had ever experienced before.

That day I telephoned Ephraim and told him what I had experienced with the Lord. The community still had reservations about considering a German foundation. What I proposed to him was if, after prayer with other senior members of the community, they still felt there was to be no house of the Lion of Juda in Germany, would he send me people for a year to help me establish a community? And to this Ephraim said yes.

I also telephoned Maria and told her of my experiences of

the last several days, and that I had said yes to the Lord; that I had agreed to take the responsibility for founding a community. I further told her of my conversation with Ephraim and that I personally believed the foundation would be a new house for the Lion of Juda. She, in turn, was continuing her efforts to begin a community herself. We appeared to be going our separate ways.

I remained *constantly* under a strong anointing from Sunday morning for a total of five days and nights, knowing inside of me that everything had already been accomplished. In the past, anointings had come over me usually only during times of ministry; this time the anointing never left me. I did not see in my spirit just one new foundation but others as well, scattered across the German-speaking countries. Thus did God give me a boldness to step out. He also seemed to be saying that he had prepared other hearts for the venture of a new community in Germany and that others would help move the project along step by step.

On the Tuesday morning Maria phoned me and said she believed she had misinterpreted some of the Lord's guidance for her; she added that she felt now that her path toward community was to be with me.

In this period I wrote a long, detailed report on my recent spiritual experience and sent it to Ephraim in English and a French translation to my bishop, Mgr Chabbèrt, for their discernment.

My schedule called for me to be in France in October. I looked forward to this trip with intense interest and expectation, because on the twenty-first of the month I would meet with Ephraim at the community's house at Mortain. When I found myself face to face with the founder of the Lion of Juda, I recounted in detail the powerful experience I had had with the Lord pointing to the establishing of the community in the German-speaking countries. My heart leapt when I heard Ephraim's response. His answer to the question of whether the Lion of Juda would be open to doing a foundation in Germany was . . . yes.

Two days later I met with Mgr Chabbèrt near Lourdes.

He gave me his permission to pursue the living out of my vision, but with a provision: in his judgment I was not called to a contemplative lifestyle, such as living in a community house and having daily responsibilities there. Rather, he said, I was called to an apostolic lifestyle of travel and ministry in many places. And he shared with me the text of the sending out of the disciples in Luke 9.1–6. His reading of this text confirmed in my heart what I felt the Lord had already showed me.

Looking back I realised that throughout my entire walk with the Lord, the impulses I felt I was receiving from God had always been submitted to those the Lord had placed in authority over me. I had moved only in obedience to their discernment. The more I grow in my understanding of obedience in spiritual matters, the more I appreciate its God-given role in the building of the Body of Christ on earth. There is a strong scriptural injunction in this regard in Hebrews 13.7: 'Obey your leaders and submit to their authority. They keep watch over you as men who must give an account. Obey them so that their work will be a joy, not a burden, for that would be of no advantage to you.'

I called Maria and told her that I had Ephraim's accord for a German house of the Lion of Juda and had just received my bishop's permission to participate in its founding. She in turn notified her superiors that she was resigning her post, and the effective date was set for January.

I also called Fr Norbert Baumert in Frankfurt. Right after my return from Ars, I had discussed with him the possibility of bringing the Lion of Juda to Germany. Now I also told him the developments of the last few days. 'I know God has a house for the community,' I told Norbert. 'We just need to find out where.'

Over the next several months Maria, Fr Norbert Baumert and I looked at a variety of houses in various parts of Germany, especially in the dioceses of Limburg and Mainz. As we spoke with authorities in different dioceses about the community, we encountered several humorous problems.

One problem was how to explain that the Lion of Juda houses brought together priests, monks, nuns, single people and married couples and their children. It sounded to these authorities like a very complicated kind of house to develop and run. Another problem was explaining that the community lived 'by faith'. It sometimes seemed as hard to explain as my efforts to persuade my sons long ago that 'God will provide for us'. People would say, 'Yes, all right; but where does the money come from?'

In December it was once again time for our family reunion. Except that this time, instead of my flying to the United States, Robert and Darin came to Europe. And our family was starting to enlarge; Robert brought along with him his fiancée, Jennifer. Their wedding was set for June of the following year.

During the Christmas-New Year holiday I read the life of Teresa of Avila. I was quite captivated by her story and felt that the Lord, through this reading, was encouraging me in the effort to establish a community in Germany. St Teresa, a Spanish Carmelite, had tried to found her community in poverty, without any major endowments. She met with great resistance, however, because this was simply not the way things were done in her day; typically, wealthy families would endow a new convent or monastery, thus attaching themselves to the power of the community's prayers. Lion of Juda houses, too, were always founded 'on faith': that is, with a minimum of resources and no human assurances of funds for the future.

Maria entered the community in France at the Lion of Juda's house in Mortain in mid-February with the specific purpose of participating in the German foundation now on the horizon. The Wednesday before Easter, just after I had finished a tour of ministry in France, I received a call saying that Maria was to be received into the community as a postulant, along with other new members, at the house in St Broladre. I quickly found a train to get me there. I was thus able to watch as the first vocation for the German house took her place in the community.

Not long after that, in April, very spontaneously, the ministry received the gift of a six-year-old Volkswagen Golf. This came in response to prayers that I might have a car to use for ministry in Europe. I now found myself the owner of a bright orange Golf with red and black racing stripes!

Soon after receiving the car I had to go to the Lion of Juda's Monastery of Marthe and Maria of Bethany near Orleans, in France, for a meeting of 'shepherds' (leaders) of the various foundations. The shepherds assemble at least once a year, and Ephraim had asked me if I would come and share with them the vision God had given me for the community in Germany. It would, after all, be from the existing houses that men and women would be drawn to form the first group for the German house. As I shared the vision I could see how the Lord was touching hearts to communicate that vision into the individual communities of the Lion of Juda so that those who felt called to this pioneering effort in Germany would be emboldened to step forward.

Driving back to Germany I asked myself why it was taking so long to find our house. Then it was as if the Holy Spirit broke into my ponderings to place this impression on my heart: 'Can I not give you a house in one day as I have given you a car? Do I not also have the vocations prepared for the house as I had said?' I knew by these impressions that God was reminding me to rest in him, to trust him, to let go of all my human frets and leave the project in his hands. So I did 'let go' and received a fresh conviction that all was well.

37

'Weep and mourn'

I attended another national Lutheran charismatic conference in May of that year, the same conference with which I had begun my ministry in the German-speaking countries in 1982. This time the meeting was in Cologne, and there, quite unexpectedly, I had a very deep experience. I had been Catholic about eighteen months and had thus far not been present for a communion service of another part of the Lord's Body. What I had previously practised during my ministry among the various parts of the Body was to ask permission to receive communion wherever I was. I had thought, in my early years of ministry, that when Christians could come together at the Lord's table, could share in the breaking of the bread, *then* we would truly be one. As I grew in understanding, however, I had indeed come to realise that there were significant differences of interpretation in the theologies of Eucharist among various Christian churches. I also began to see that just to brush aside those differences, to act as if they did not matter, would not produce a true unity, but rather a flawed and superficial 'togetherness'. In addition, if I went against the guidelines of my own church in the matter of 'inter-communion', I would also be breaking the unity between myself and the church in which God had placed me. I could not, after all, treat the Eucharist as something that belonged to me as an individual to do with it whatever I liked.

Thus, when time came for communion to be distributed to those sharing the platform in Cologne, as a Catholic, I was not able to partake of it. My heart just broke and I started to weep. I wept and wept and wept, openly, in front of all, feeling as I did the pain of the division between Lutherans and Catholics.[70]

---

[70] As Alan Schreck writes: 'Catholics cannot in good conscience join with other Christians in this "sacrament of unity" while there still remains a basic disunity and disagreement with them about the Eucharist itself, and about other important points of Christian faith. Catholics understand participation in the Eucharist primarily as the ultimate sign of the unity that exists among Christians, rather than as a means for achieving unity . . . Catholics earnestly wish to seek reconciliation with other Christians, both as individuals and churches, so that we will be able to approach the altar of God together in genuine unity of mind and heart.' *Catholic and Christian*, pp135–136. There are other theological arguments about Eucharist having a primary sign value.

Having to say no on that day, having to experience the pain and the breaking in my heart, along with the tears that just flooded and flooded, and the love I had for my Lutheran brothers and sisters, I also received a renewed burning of my heart to intercede before the throne of God for the healing of his torn and divided Body.

And again the words of the Kansas City prophecy rang through my heart: *Weep and mourn, for the Body of My Son is broken.*

A very special event drew me to the United States in June: the wedding of my son Robert to Jennifer. Arriving four days before the wedding I settled into Robert's apartment, the place to which he would soon bring his bride. I plunged into cleaning everything from top to bottom and tried in other ways to help my son with the final details.

On a Saturday afternoon I watched with pride as Jennifer came down the aisle in her beautiful white gown, trailing a long train, and joined my son at the altar. They were joined in the holy sacrament of marriage in the Catholic parish where Jennifer had attended church most of her life. As I looked at the two of them standing side by side before the altar, I lifted praises of thanks to my Lord for his goodness in their lives.

38

Haus Aspel

Back to Europe by mid July, I attended the Lion of Juda's annual praise and worship session at Ars, then returned to my home base in Germany to resume, with Maria, the search for the house. By this point we had three or four houses in mind and our plan was to visit each of them during the first part of August.

It was in this period that we first saw Haus Aspel, a large complex of the Daughters of the Holy Cross situated close to

Rees in the Diocese of Muenster in northern Germany, near the Dutch border. The complex contained a large, recently vacated high school building, the sisters' convent and a 90-bed retreat centre, with beautifully landscaped grounds and even a small lake.

Our visit came on August 6. We were able to tour the complex and grounds, and answer the sisters' questions about the Community of the Lion of Juda. From that day forward things moved quickly. The next day we visited the bishop's office, since the Lion of Juda never moves into a diocese without the bishop's welcome. Though the bishop himself was on vacation, our contacts with his administrative staff went smoothly.

In our hearts, Maria and I were still not sure if what we had discovered corresponded to the Lord's plans for the community. But as soon as Ephraim saw the pictures of the school building and other descriptive material, he said he felt, in the Spirit, that that building at Haus Aspel was indeed the place that God was calling us to occupy. So we went ahead with additional meetings to pave the way for the establishing of the community's first foundation in Germany, and its twentieth house in all.

39

Belfast

Soon afterward, the ninth meeting of the European Ecumenical Charismatic Leaders group was held in Rostrevor, Northern Ireland, and, as a member, I attended it. Ireland! Yet another place that so poignantly symbolised the division in the Body. Indeed, it had been planned that while the leaders group were together in that strife-torn country, we might go to Belfast to meet with Christians, both Catholics and Protestants, who were working and praying together for reconciliation and unity.

Ireland, emerald isle so plagued by division and violence —a violence that was to reach out and touch me personally. The night before our group went from Rostrevor to Belfast by chartered bus, a young Catholic man was shot in the back and killed as he was leaving a prayer meeting in Belfast. The assailants were three Protestants. The victim was in his early thirties, a father of four children.

The next day, while I was with the leaders' group in Belfast, there was a retaliatory killing of a Protestant man. I could feel the heaviness in the air. The same afternoon we met with the Roman Catholic bishop and with the moderator of the Presbyterian Church of Ireland, who both briefed us on the state of tension and on dialogues under way aimed at reducing it.

Riding back to the centre where our meeting was taking place, I heard again resounding in my heart the words: *Weep and mourn, for the Body of My Son is broken.*

The next morning in prayer, as I was still feeling the heaviness from the two killings, I sensed in my spirit that the Lord wanted to take me deeper in an understanding of a painful spiritual truth. It was as if Jesus were saying to me, 'You've looked around, and what have you seen? You've seen what division has done in this land, and you've seen the fruits of that division—death.[71] But do you realise what the division in my Body has meant? Do you realise how many spiritual deaths have occurred because my Body is broken?'

It was very difficult to think of anything besides the impression of those words upon my heart. I realised that I had been called to be an instrument of healing in the midst of division, an instrument of life, to convey Jesus and his love, in the midst of death and ruin.

As the European Ecumenical Charismatic Leaders meeting drew to a close, we weighed the usual question of whether God wanted us to meet again. After prayer and reflection, we concluded that we should hold a tenth meeting. The place would be Berlin, the time September 1988. I felt in my spirit

---

[71] See Romans 6.23.

that the Lord would do something extraordinary with the leaders' group at that tenth meeting. I also had an inner awareness that it was not by chance that God was moving us from one divided country, Ireland, to another, Germany, and to a divided city within that country.

Since the host country normally undertook the responsibility of organising the meeting, Gunter Oppermann and I volunteered to prepare the Berlin conference. I left Ireland with a feeling that God's Spirit was soon going to blow across Europe with new intensity.

40

'Missio' and missions

Meanwhile, things were developing rapidly toward the founding of the first Lion of Juda house in Germany. Sister Hélène, a nun, had been chosen to be the shepherd of the new foundation. In her ten years in the community this would be the fourth time that she had participated in the beginning of a house. Her last four years had been spent in the house in Zaïre, which was where I had first met her. The Lord had also touched the hearts of two couples in the community, Yves and Marie-Noelle, who had three children, and another couple that had been married for just a few months, Philippe and Catherine. Sister Hélène, Yves and Marie-Noelle came to live at the house in Mortain with Maria, doing what they could to prepare the community's move into Germany. They translated many of the community's liturgies—prayers and songs—into German. Also during this period several sisters of the Daughters of the Holy Cross went to France to see the community's house at Mortain and to meet with Ephraim.

I joined with sister Hélène and Maria in meeting the Bishop of Muenster, Bernhard Lettmann, and with the

Provincial Superior of the Daughters of the Holy Cross, at Haus Aspel in mid-October.

At last, on November 3, the vision I had experienced and had kept in my heart became a reality: the Community of the Lion of Juda arrived to install itself in the former school building in the complex at Haus Aspel. They arrived to a basically empty building, a place with no furnishings at all. Within weeks after the community's arrival, however, from various parts of Germany, a steady flow of furniture trickled into the house. On November 12 I was present for a time of prayer in the temporary chapel of the new foundation, and I could see with my eyes, finally, that which I had seen in my spirit. Once again I joyously praised the Lord for his faithfulness, and for the way he encouraged in the face of delays and obstacles.

On another level God was actively at work integrating my ministry into the life of the Catholic church in Europe and, in effect, providing me with references for ministry, both within the Catholic church and, more broadly, within various ecumenical charismatic circles. In September 1985 Mgr Chabbèrt had written a 'missio' (statement of sending forth) for my work. In this missio he acknowledged my reception into the Catholic church and assented to the ministry of evangelisation which I had felt led to carry out, especially in the context of ecumenical efforts toward Christian unity. He also recommended me to the priests for ministry, stating that 'in her we perceive an inspired decision for the church, true spiritual life, and also a passionate eagerness to proclaim Christ'.

This mission would be favourably received in January 1986 by the Bishop of Limburg, Germany, in whose diocese I had maintained a guest room for the past three years.

At the same time as the Lion of Juda was taking up residence in Germany, I also received news that I had been elected to the National Council of the Catholic Charismatic Renewal in that country. Later I was also voted on to its co-ordinating group.

The vote seemed to reinforce my growing impression I belonged in Germany, the land of my family roots and my family blood. God, I felt, was allowing my identification with Germany to deepen, and, for the time being, the question of where my physical home was, of what country I should live in, appeared to be resolved.

As 1986 was drawing to a close, Christmas again beckoned me back to the United States for a reunion with my sons and my daughter-in-law. The intensity of my life in this year had been such that I welcomed the arrival of the Christmas holidays with great anticipation of rest and refreshment. Soon after my arrival in the States, however, I fell ill with a viral infection.

Upon my return to Germany I tried at first to meet my schedule, but found I could not do so entirely. I would be all right for a day, then would find myself back in bed, then up again, then back down with pain and complications. This pattern continued for about seven weeks.

Visiting Haus Aspel I found the community busily engaged in renovation of the school building. It had only large classrooms, with no individual rooms for sleeping at all. Much had to be done to turn the structure into a real 'house' for the Lion of Juda. In every house of the community, the first place to be remodelled, or created if it does not already exist, is the chapel. And the chapel was exactly what everybody was working on. As members of the house opened the doors for me on a January morning that I might see the work already done to create the house's chapel, I took a step backward in astonishment. With the wall gone and the two rooms made into one large room, I found myself back in my vision of September 1985; that is, back in the dream I had had in which I saw myself opening a door and saying to two others, 'This room will be our chapel.' The room I was staring at now was exactly the same room I had seen in my dream.

The regional bishop, Mgr Hans Jansen, came to Haus Aspel on February 2 to celebrate Mass for the community and to bless our chapel. The chapel overflowed with more than 120 people present to share this occasion with us. It was also at this point that we felt God calling us to name our house in the Haus Aspel complex 'St Michael', after the archangel who, faithful to the Lord, battled with Lucifer and his legions and hurled them from heaven into hell.

One day I found myself without a translator. I had been making progress in the German language, using it frequently now for one-to-one conversations; but I did not feel secure enough to speak German while teaching or praying with groups. God, I felt, had other ideas; he seemed to be telling me to be willing, in my weakness, to speak German while I ministered, and to trust him to supply the words. I asked the Lord to confirm this impression somehow. That very morning a prophetic word was spoken during the Mass: 'Do not be afraid.' It felt in my heart that that was all the confirmation that I needed.

That afternoon I was scheduled to speak to a group of young people. As I approached the time of sharing with them I found my knees shaking. My heart was beating so strongly I thought that others, surely, could hear it. Somehow I managed to get through the session with the young people in halting, error-ridden German.

After I finished I retired to a prayer room that had been set aside for me. I began to lament in my spirit, saying things such as, 'Oh, Lord, how I wish that my command of German had been better so that I could have expressed the theme on forgiveness more deeply.' My heart was still beating very rapidly. Then the Lord broke in and began to shed some light on the true state of my spirit. He showed me that what was hurting me was not really that I hadn't been able to teach at a deeper level, but rather that my pride was suffering from my having had to stand up and speak publicly in broken German.

Feelings of pride continued to be a hindrance to me in months to follow as the Lord kept encouraging me to speak out in German when I stood to minister. I was constantly having to battle with the fear of what other people might think of me, caught between my pride in not wanting to speak German in public until I had perfected my use of it and my obedience to do as the Lord was calling me to do, even if that meant playing the fool.[72] This was one of the ways in which God invited me to get out of my boat and, relying on his power, walk on water. In various ways he is calling upon all of us to do the same; relying on what we are humanly capable of doing will not be enough once we embark on a journey with the Lord.

The Haus Aspel complex contained a large retreat house, run by the Daughters of the Holy Cross. Our new community just installed there had felt called to schedule an Easter retreat, open to all, on the theme 'Jesus is risen!' Fr Norbert Baumert and I were to lead the retreat. We had reserved the retreat house and every bed had been filled. There were also over thirty young people camped on the floors of the community's house. They had simply put down sleeping bags or mattresses in the large classrooms.

In addition we were to enter into the Easter celebration with the priest who serves as chaplain to the Daughters of the Holy Cross, with the sisters themselves and with those from the neighbourhood who, year by year, usually came to the Easter liturgy at Haus Aspel. In short, we were to see four different streams of the Catholic faith, merging charismatics and non-charismatics, flowing together to proclaim the Lord's resurrection that Easter.

After we had celebrated the Easter Vigil service on Saturday evening, we all went together into the gymnasium, a separate building behind our house; only in the gymnasium was there enough room to accommodate all of us. Inside, the room was very festively decorated, with many, many arrangements of candles and flowers. Everyone joined in sharing food and drink, and to enjoy what in Protestant

---

[72] I felt led by the Holy Spirit to use German in assemblies for almost a year. There came a point, however, where I felt He was giving me the liberty to teach through translation or to teach directly in German, as I felt best according to each circumstance.

circles is known as 'fellowship'. The buzz of dozens of happy conversations brought the gymnasium alive. Then a member of the Lion of Juda began to play on an organ some of the traditional Israeli spiritual songs, with lyrics from the Old Testament. The songs are conceived as music for dances. Not only did the charismatics enter into dancing unto the Lord, but so did the Daughters of the Holy Cross and lay people from the neighbourhood.

I got up on a chair and watched in awe the scene unfolding before my eyes: the joyful praise of the Lord's resurrection, the Lion of Juda concretely established now in Germany, and in the heart of the Catholic church in this particular diocese, the retreatants, young people, nuns and people from the neighbourhood all singing and dancing together.

On Sunday the weather warmed enough for us to go outside for Easter dinner at mid-day. And, as is the custom in houses of the community, tables and chairs were paraded outdoors all the while the cooking of a large dinner was being accomplished. Again, I stood to the side and watched in awe as people passed me carrying chairs and dishes. I was absolutely exhuberant watching the spirit of the community, so free and contagious, taking root in this new place that God had prepared for us in Germany. My heart felt as if it would burst from sheer joy.

In May 1987 International Catholic Charismatic Leaders met in Rome and I attended as a representative from Germany. Every country where the Catholic Renewal is present had been given the opportunity to send representatives. In all, about a thousand leaders arrived in Rome from every part of the globe.

And there, in Rome, rather than in the United States, I had my first contact with fellow Americans who were serving the Catholic Renewal in the States. It seemed very strange to me that I should not, somehow, have met them before this.

Moreover, as I walked among representatives from so many different lands, a restlessness arose in my heart. It seemed that I could not truly identify with any one country at all, not with Germany, not with the United States. Where was home?

In our sharing groups we were invited to divide ourselves up according to the languages we spoke. I thus had a choice to make between German and English, and I chose English. In my group there were leaders from the Philippines, from Japan, from Austria, from Canada, and from different African nations. It was really exciting to listen to the ways in which the Lord was pouring out his Spirit in various lands and in which his life was permeating into the hearts that were open to his Spirit.

During this meeting all the leaders were received together by Pope John Paul II in a special audience. I was especially impressed by the peace and strength I saw reflected in his face.

I had one other very memorable experience during this visit to Rome, something that was organised quite spontaneously. The leaders' group discovered that our meeting coincided with a meeting of superiors of women's orders, and that the nuns' leaders' group was to be addressed by Mother Teresa. The charismatic leaders quickly got in touch with Mother Teresa and worked it out for her to speak to our group as well. The theme on which our meeting had been focused was 'good news to the poor'. Indeed, we had by this point heard from many different perspectives bearing on this theme, spiritual, sociological, political, economic. I had heard much about the Albanian-born nun who had developed such a dramatic ministry to the poor in India and elsewhere, and I felt that if there was any one person in the world who really understood about poverty, it was she. The simple words ignited in Mother Teresa's heart that day by the fire of the Holy Spirit touched my own heart deeply. 'The poor,' she said, 'are those, wherever they are in the world, who do not know Jesus Christ. Whether they have material wealth or not means nothing if they do not have Christ in their lives.' She also made it plain that, very likely, there were many 'poor people' in our own families.

41

Darkness

After the meeting in Rome, while back in Germany, I entered into a very difficult period, a time unlike any I had ever known before: my first real spiritual desert. Ever since I had found my way back to the Lord I had experienced strong rays of light from the Holy Spirit, illuminating the path that I felt God had called me to walk. And I had walked with a deep knowledge in my heart of the various steps to which God appeared to be calling me. I knew that God had prepared the way, that God was revealing himself to me through his Spirit. Now, suddenly, on May 20, everything within me went dark. Every vision that had previously been illuminated, that had even burned brightly in my spirit, seemed to have vanished.

As I moved through my schedule of ministry, every time I would stand to preach, teach or pray for others, the Holy Spirit would be there to meet me. But inwardly, for myself personally, there was no feeling of life. I began to rationalise over what was taking place. 'You're just tired,' I told myself. 'You have been under tremendous emotional strain in the ministry and in the effort to found the community, and you are simply worn out.' I had also gone six months now without anyone to help me with the administrative side of the ministry, and so had had to handle secretarial chores on my own.

What was happening, however, it soon became obvious, was that Satan and his cohorts had launched a strong spiritual attack on me and on the ministry. The enemy was using considerable force to try to block understandings and events that God was trying to bring forth.

A weekend gathering including over a hundred community members from different houses of the Lion of Juda had been planned for Haus Aspel for June 12–14. Ephraim and his wife Jo were to be among the participants. It was conceived as a time of blessing and celebration in thanksgiving for the Lord's work in the founding of the community in Germany. This was a weekend I had long looked forward to. But when it arrived, I was in bed in the guest room in central Germany, alone, sick, too weak to travel. I felt enveloped in darkness.

In this sad state I had to prepare myself to take part in the first national meeting of the Catholic Charismatic Renewal to be held in Germany in four years. One year earlier I had perceived in my heart that God would pour out great blessings on this meeting, that we would see virtually a 'breakthrough' in the release of the Holy Spirit's power for renewal. And now there was no light, there were no feelings; everything was just dark. I dreaded even thinking about going to this meeting, which was to be held in Friedrichshafen. I knew that I had various duties to perform there, however, and so after spending a week in bed, I pulled myself together and went.

When I arrived I asked a brother and a sister if they would pray for me. I asked them to pray to break the hold of the powers of darkness that I had by now perceived had had a hand in what I was going through.

On the morning of June 17, all at once, God's brilliant radiance pierced and dispersed the dark clouds that had been cloaking my spirit. Light suddenly broke through and reilluminated within me every single vision I had ever carried, including the vision for the Friedrichshafen meeting. The knowledge of what God was going to do just filled my heart. The sensation was explosive.

I was alive! I was one—spirit, mind and body!

'I've broken through!' I exclaimed to several people around me.

As the congress began, on June 18, I entered into it with a knowledge of the tenderness and the greatness of the Father's love.

God had opened many doors for the Lion of Juda to participate in the Friedrichshafen meeting, even though the community was very young in Germany. Not only did we have members of the German house present, but also

German-speaking brothers and sisters from other houses, so that, all together, the Lion of Juda had about twenty members taking part. We were invited to lead the singing of morning praises each day, and also to present ourselves as a community in a workshop on communal Christian living. Then the community was given the charge of a blessing service. The moderator-general of the community, Dr Philippe Madré, a married Catholic deacon, and his wife, Evelyne, came from France to lead this service.

42

As one

On the 'prayer ministry' team,[73] in which I participated, the Lord gave us a marvellous unity, a oneness that enabled us to be really open to the outpouring of his power and love through the gifts of the Spirit.

One plan for the congress was that on Saturday night, we would take all the participants on large boats and sail out onto the Bodensee. At a certain point on the vast lake, we would join together in praising the Lord. The weather on Friday, however, was rainy, and there was quite a chill in the air. On Saturday morning the weather report looked even grimmer.

The whole organisational team now knew in their hearts that we were *not* to go out on the lake and separate from each other by being in different boats. Rather, all felt that the Lord was calling us to stay together in the conference centre for that Saturday evening. Once this alternative was proposed to the entire assembly, the applause that broke out

---

[73] A team of people who have been selected by the organisers to sit on, or near, the platform and be available for special prayer needs or the manifestation of the gifts of the Holy Spirit, as the Lord leads.

confirmed that God had already brought the hearts of the participants into accord.

But God was only beginning with us. He wanted to show us *why* he wanted us all together, united in Jesus.

Father Ernst Sievers is a White Father from Germany who had served in Africa but had been back in his homeland for the past three years working with the Renewal. He would soon be leaving to go to Uganda to head the Renewal there. He shared in his teaching that the Holy Spirit was calling us to be empowered to go forth as witnesses for God's kingdom on earth. He cited Ezekiel 37.5, 'I will make breath enter you, and you will come to life.'

Then came Father Tom Forrest. An American priest who had served the Renewal for many years in Latin America, he had, until 1984, been chairman of the International Catholic Charismatic Renewal Office. He had recently initiated and was currently directing a project called 'Evangelisation 2,000', with offices in Rome.

He very simply shared with us in Friedrichshafen a vision that he felt God had placed on his heart—a vision of a world 'more Christian than not: an absolute majority of the human race converted to Christianity by the year 2000.'

According to St Thomas Aquinas the phenomenon of a 'personal Pentecost' was the norm for all Christians in the first century, Fr Forrest told the Friedrichshafen congress. He added that, not even counting members of Pentecostal churches, 'there are tens of millions of people alive today who are telling the story of their own personal Pentecost.

'And Pentecost is for *evangelisation*.

'In June 1984 I wrote a rather long letter to the Pope. In that letter I asked Pope John Paul to declare a "decade of evangelisation"—ten years in which all Catholics, and all other Christians, unite in doing one thing: to give Jesus what he wants—a Christian world.'

A twentieth-century 'kairos'

As Fr Forrest was speaking, more and more of the Spirit's light flooded into my heart, illuminating the details of a picture that God had been painting in my heart over the last five years. It was like seeing the piecing together of a mosaic—a picture of the healing of the Lord's divided and torn Body. Even though I now could glimpse only a few of its details, it was a mosaic that I knew intuitively would, in the years ahead, consume my life.

Continuing in his talk, Fr Forrest declared: 'In the New Testament there is a special Greek word for a special kind of time: *kairos*. Now kairos is a God-graced moment. It is a God-prepared moment. Abraham had a kairos when God spoke to him in a vision and made a covenant with him. Moses had a kairos when God called him to free his people Israel. A young girl had a kairos when an angel of God proclaimed that she would be the mother of the Messiah.

'I believe with all my heart and soul that everything that Christianity has experienced in this century, everything that Catholics have experienced through this glorious outpouring of the Holy Spirit, is God's preparation of *our* kairos.

'Catholic Charismatic Renewal is now twenty years old. When you are twenty years old, it is time to stop being a child and become a man or a woman of God. Time to fulfil your mission on earth.

'In the plans being developed for a decade of evangelisation leading up to the year 2000, we must work to stop all the childish divisions in the church. We don't have time for Catholics arguing with Catholics. We don't have time for Christians arguing with Christians. We only have time for the work of evangelisation.

'No one who does not evangelise is free to say, "I am a good Christian".'

Fr Forrest went on to mention that the Second Vatican

Council said that 'evangelisation is the most basic task of the people of God'. He also cited the encyclical *Evangelii Nuntiandi* ('Evangelisation in the Modern World') by Pope Paul VI, which insisted: 'The Church exists to evangelise.'

He went on: 'I ask people everywhere, "Are you the people of God?" And they say, "Yes." Then I say, "Must the people of God evangelise?" And they say, "Yes." Then I say, "Do you know *how* to evangelise?" And they say, "No." This is terrible. The church does not know how to do what it exists to do!'

'To give Jesus Christ the present of a Christian world,' he continued, 'we must start by praying and fasting, as well as by doing penance.' Little children must pray, the sick must pray, the suffering, the old and the young must pray . . .

'And after we pray, we must wait and listen, to find out what our own job in this great task is to be. Pray and listen! God created you, knowing in his heart exactly how he planned to use you—*every single one of you*.

'I'm not suggesting a work of man, however; I'm suggesting *a work of God, a work of the Holy Spirit*, in this century that has seen the greatest outpouring of the Holy Spirit ever known.'

That afternoon the programme called for an ecumenical forum of ten participants, Baptist, Catholic, Interdenominational, Lutheran, and Reformed. There we were on the platform together, members of different parts of the Lord's body, sharing experiences and perspectives on the theme of 'Spiritual Awakening in Germany and in the World' and praying together. What I felt the Holy Spirit wanted me to express was that without unity, there would be no real awakening. I also posed once again the question, 'Do you love Jesus?' and told the assembly that that question had to be linked to another, 'Do you love his church?' 'It is very hard to love the Head without loving the Body, too,' I said.

The Lord's love which radiated upon us in the large convention centre that Saturday afternoon could virtually be felt through our senses. We felt a joy in being there together as God's children: united in Christ, recognising, nonetheless, our differences, but receiving one another in love in the midst of those differences.

Following an impulse of the Holy Spirit, a time of worship began in the large congress hall. Many people were plainly expectant that God would transform their hearts. We started with a pantomime and then, before the Holy Sacrament had adoration and spiritual dance performed by a dance team. We then had a period of community prayer in which we were asked to renounce things in our lives that were not of the Lord. Then, led by Fr Ernst Sievers, we opened our hearts for a fresh outpouring of the Holy Spirit and a release of the Spirit's gifts.

As we began a spontaneous 'clap offering' to the Lord, Fr Sievers told us that in places where he had served in Africa, Christians clapped for God with their hands over their heads. Suddenly, in response, everyone began to clap with hands held over heads, and as I looked out over the throng of four thousand, it looked as if flames of fire were flickering over people's heads, all over the auditorium.

The breakthrough that I had waited for for so long—the breakthrough of God's glory and anointing, giving the Spirit liberty to move as he desired—I was now seeing all around me in the Friedrichshafen congress.

On Sunday morning I had breakfast with Fr Tom Forrest. I told him of the vision and hope I had been holding in my heart for the European Ecumenical Charismatic Leaders meeting scheduled for September 1988 in Berlin. The meeting's theme was to be 'Evangelisation—Unity—Renewal'. 'I believe,' I told him, 'that this meeting is part of God's plan for getting Europe ready to respond to the call for the decade of evangelisation.' And I invited him to come to Berlin as a speaker. Then he gave me details of a worldwide ecumenical charismatic leaders meeting, the Singapore Consultation, the previous February. The meeting brought together about fifty leaders from different Christian bodies to pray and consult together about world evangelisation. The group had scheduled a second meeting for February 1988, also in Singapore.

'When Catholics, Pentecostals and Protestants from all

over the world meet together,' Fr Forrest commented, 'instant harmony is not something one can take for granted. Yet that is what happened when we met in Singapore.'

Fr Forrest had asked all of us in Friedrichshafen to pray and listen—and God would reveal to each of us our part in the decade of evangelisation.

As I prayed and listened, I was swept up almost immediately in a flurry of activity.

Within a week I was asked to join a second European leaders group in Europe that had developed following the Strasbourg congress. I felt God was saying, 'Yes, join,' and that he would be drawing both leaders' groups together in Berlin, that the groups be no longer two but one.

In early September I took a train to Bern, Switzerland, to attend my first meeting with the second European leaders group, who numbered about thirty. The discussion there focused on mounting a Charismatic European Leaders Congress to inspire, encourage, and train willing Christians for the task of evangelisation. This congress was set for July 1990 in Bern to launch Europe's part of a decade of evangelisation.

Following this three-day session, the Catholic representatives in Bern decided it would be good to have a Catholic member of the group visit Rome to brief key Catholic leaders about the plans for the congress. It was agreed that I should be sent. The only time in my schedule I had free was a three-day period five days from then. I thought it would be next to impossible to set up the necessary appointments at such short notice, but, astonishingly, after just three telephone calls, all appointments had been made. And I was off to Rome, where all the meetings went well.

Amid a relentlessly intense schedule of ministry in autumn 1987, I took a welcome pause in early November to help the community at Haus Aspel celebrate their first anniversary. Coinciding with these festivities was the baptism of the first baby born into the German community, Joseph, the son of Philippe and Catherine Timmel. I became the baby's godmother. Auspiciously, the community had doubled in size and now numbered twelve adults and seven children.

WHERE IS HOME?

A perception was already growing in the community that we should be open to the establishing of a second foundation somewhere in the German-speaking countries. And, indeed, word soon began to filter in about various large houses that might be available. When God's hour arrived, we all knew, another house would be started.

Besides the streams of evangelistic ministry and community, though, my life had by now also flowed into a third stream, that of participation in both German and European committees on the Charismatic Renewal. That third stream, I soon learned, was to become increasingly international. Shortly after the second Singapore Consultation I received a letter from one of the participants telling me that I would soon be sent an official invitation to join that group for nine days of intensive prayer and discussion in Jerusalem over Pentecost 1989. He said the group was to expand to some 120 people, all leaders in the worldwide Charismatic Renewal.

The group's aim is to develop a network of 5,000–10,000 leaders spread around the globe and train them as dynamic catalysts for evangelising the world before the year 2000. All these leaders are then to be invited to gather for a Charismatic World Leaders Congress in 1991.

The week that the official invitation from the Singapore Consultation arrived in April my schedule had me in Paris, where I spent an evening in prayer with two friends.

Suddenly, the Lord gave us a very strong prophetic vision about the urgency of the hour. In my spirit I could see dark clouds descending on cities as if to smother their inhabitants in confusion and fear. I felt that the Lord had been trying to shake us awake and show us the spiritual warfare going on all around us: that we are in an hour in which the enemy, with well-laid plans, was unleashing his forces to snare the earth's peoples in the esoteric traps of 'new age' movements—occultism, spiritism, witchcraft, magic, drugs, pleasure-seeking, and much more; that the Holy Spirit is challenging us as Christians to unite and rally, and go forth boldly in his power, proclaiming Christ.

I perceived, however, that serious hindrances were

keeping us from rising to this challenge. That many of us are still comfortable with secret sin, hidden from others' view deep in our hearts. That, comfortable with the Lord's grace and mercy, some of us are seeking only forgiveness for those sins, not deliverance from them. Compromise with sin, I felt the Lord was showing me, would cause many either to fail to respond to the battle call, or to stumble and fall in the fray.

Three times the words resounded, 'Protect your hearts and keep them pure!' The Lord is challenging all believers to a greater holiness and transparency of heart. The vision brought us an inner knowledge of how crucial this was for the fight. Only transparent hearts can convey the light of Christ that we need, to stand on the front lines of battle and hurl back the enemy.

Over the cities, I began to see, rays of light were piercing the darkness as the church threw herself into the assault. The battle was fierce. Nonetheless, I felt impressed upon my heart, 'Fear not, I am with you.'

I also had an awareness that God was issuing a call to maturity. I saw that this meant, in part, growing out of our self-centred spiritualities in which we come before God mainly to meet our own needs, questing after our own wholeness. Did Jesus not tell us, 'If anyone would come after me, he must deny himself, take up his cross and follow me'? It struck me then that this kind of radical discipleship was now the only way left to us. And as we responded to the Lord's call to obedience, he would meet us with his grace and power and make us whole.

As the vision concluded, I felt my entire being reverberate with an awareness of how urgent the hour has become, and of how great the task is that lies before us. But we do not go forth alone. All the wisdom and the power of the Lord is with us—and the more so as we learn to give ourselves over to Jesus in love. Once we have really surrendered ourselves to him, he will take us and use us in ways far beyond the poor powers of our own imaginings.

For I believe he is still saying to his church: 'Of that which I intend to do in your midst, it is only the beginning.'